The 90-Day Thought Leader

A Practical Playbook

Bryon J. Casler

Director of Product • Process Engineer • Visionary & Leader • LSBB • PMP • SPOC

Life Studies: Psychology, Philosophy, Theology, Statistical Probabilities

Dedication

For those who believe they have something worth saying — and the courage to say it.

Table of Contents

Introduction

The Guru Parade

The internet has taught me two things: cats secretly run the algorithm, and everyone seems to be a guru. Open any feed, and it feels like you've stumbled into a never-ending parade. Here comes the "LinkedIn ninja" with his polished videos, the "Instagram prophet" with a perfectly curated life, and the "productivity wizard" who claims to wake up at 4 a.m. to read three books before sunrise. Each one waves from their float, tossing out catchy slogans like candy at a small-town festival.

At first, it's entertaining. Who doesn't love the spectacle of bright colors, bold fonts, and quick fixes wrapped in inspirational music? You lean in, thinking maybe this float has the secret. Maybe this guru has finally cracked the code on success, happiness, or leadership. But as the parade goes on, you start to notice something: the candy is just sugar. It looks sweet but leaves you empty.

The irony is hard to miss. Many of these self-proclaimed experts don't actually practice what they preach. It's like watching someone sell swimming lessons while reclining in a lounge chair poolside, sunscreen on, but never touching the water. Their words are loud, their megaphones polished, but their lives don't echo the clarity they promote. Noise disguised as wisdom.

I remember once stumbling across a post titled "Seven Leadership Lessons from My Goldfish." Clever title. Intriguing enough to make me click. But beneath the hook, it was nothing more than recycled platitudes dressed in novelty. "Be consistent." "Keep swimming." "Don't forget to eat." Cute, maybe, but not useful. The comments section, however, was overflowing with emojis, applause, and people proclaiming how "life-changing" it was. That's the nature of noise—it spreads faster than clarity because it doesn't require depth.

Noise is seductive because it's easy. It gives us the feeling of progress without requiring us to do the work. Share the post, save the quote, repeat the catchphrase—it all feels like growth. But real clarity isn't found in catchphrases. Clarity demands effort. It requires testing ideas in the fires of reality, not just on the bright screens of social media.

The danger is that in chasing this parade, leaders begin to mistake noise for wisdom. They consume content endlessly, hoping the next guru float will finally carry the secret they've been waiting for. But the truth is, you don't need another float. You don't need another noisy megaphone. What you need is the quiet moment away from the crowd, where clarity can whisper the truth, you've been ignoring.

True thought leadership doesn't look like a parade. It looks like consistency in the trenches. It looks like living the principles you teach, not just posting about them. The best leaders I've followed weren't shouting with a megaphone; they were walking with their teams, sleeves rolled up, figuring it out alongside them. That's not flashy. It doesn't always trend. But it leaves an impact that noise never will.

Noise entertains, but clarity transforms. The difference is simple: noise is about being seen, while clarity is about helping others see. A leader who chases noise draws attention to themselves; a leader who chooses clarity shines a light forward for others. That's the kind of leadership people remember because it changes more than the moment—it changes the direction of a life, a team, or even a community.

So, when you scroll through your feed tomorrow, ask yourself: are you joining the parade, or are you stepping aside to listen for clarity? There's nothing wrong with watching the floats pass by—but your role isn't to chase them. Your role is to build something that lasts after the parade has moved on.

Reflection Journal

What "noise" in your world feels the loudest right now?

How has it distracted you from your own clarity?

Where might you step away from the parade to find a quieter, clearer path?

[Write here]

_____

_____

_____

_____

Noise vs. Signal

Every leader faces a daily decision: will I add to the noise, or will I amplify the signal? Noise is everywhere—it's abundant, cheap, and easy to spread. Signal is rare, often buried beneath layers of distraction, waiting for someone patient enough to tune it in. The difference between the two determines whether people walk away confused or inspired.

Noise usually arrives dressed as activity. A flood of emails, endless status updates, or PowerPoint slides stuffed with text. On the surface, it looks impressive. But if you step back, you realize nothing has really been communicated. It's all static-volume without meaning. I once sat through a presentation that lasted nearly an hour, full of numbers and jargon. When the last slide clicked off, the room went quiet. Finally, someone asked the only question that mattered: "What does this mean for us today?" No one could answer. That's noise.

Signal, on the other hand, is precise. It doesn't overwhelm; it sharpens. When someone speaks with clarity, the room leans in.

People understand not just what's being said but why it matters. Signal cuts through complexity the way a radio dial locks onto a frequency. You hear it instantly: sharp, clean, undeniable.

I learned this lesson early in my career. I once sent my team a 2,000-word email outlining our goals for the quarter. I thought I was being thorough. Weeks later, I realized most people hadn't even finished reading it. Buried in all that text was one simple priority: deliver on time. If I had led with that one clear signal, the team would have aligned faster and executed better. Instead, my noise got in the way.

Noise also loves drama. It thrives in meetings that stretch too long, in conversations that circle around without landing, and in projects that generate more documentation than results. Leaders often mistake this busyness for productivity, but deep down, everyone knows it's wasted energy. It's motion without movement.

Signal, by contrast, brings energy. When clarity shows up, people rally around it. They stop guessing and start acting. Signal builds momentum because it replaces uncertainty with direction. A good leader doesn't have to shout to be heard; they simply need to speak with enough clarity that the signal resonates.

The tricky part is that noise can feel satisfying. Sharing another chart, adding another bullet point, or drafting another memo can give the illusion of control. But signal requires restraint. It asks us to say less but mean more. It challenges us to cut the excess so the essential can be seen.

Think of a radio tuner. Spin the dial fast and all you hear is static—crackling, distorted fragments of words and music. But slow down, focus, and you'll land on a frequency that comes through crisp and clear. That's the discipline of leadership: slowing down enough to find the signal in the static.

The leaders who master this aren't the ones with the most slides or the loudest voices. They're the ones who can take a swirling storm of information and name the one thing that matters. That's the kind of clarity that sticks. It doesn't just inform—it transforms.

So ask yourself: are you turning up the noise, or are you tuning into the signal? The difference determines whether the people you lead walk away distracted or walk away clear on what needs to happen next.

Where in your leadership do you find yourself adding to the static?

What is one "signal" you need to amplify more clearly for your team or family?

How can you practice tuning out noise this week to hear what truly matters?

[Write here]

_____

_____

_____

_____

Too Many Hats

Leadership often feels like running a costume shop where every role demands a new hat. One moment you're the strategist, sketching out the big picture. The next, you're the mentor, listening with empathy to someone's personal struggle. A few minutes later, you're the taskmaster, checking deadlines and ensuring details don't slip. Each hat is necessary. But try wearing them all at once, and you'll look—and feel—ridiculous.

I learned this the hard way. Early in my career, I prided myself on being versatile. If a meeting needed a visionary, I'd step up. If a spreadsheet needed fixing, I'd dive in. But somewhere along the way, my team stopped knowing who I really was. Was I the coach? The fixer? The dreamer? By trying to be everything, I ended up being unclear. And my lack of clarity spilled over to them.

Wearing too many hats at once creates confusion because people don't know which version of you they're dealing with. Imagine a meeting where you're trying to inspire your team with a bold vision while also nitpicking the font on the presentation slides. The roles clash. Instead of inspiration, you leave people frustrated.

Clarity in leadership begins with choosing the right hat for the right moment. A good leader knows when to put on the strategist cap and when to set it down to wear the mentor's cap. It's not about abandoning flexibility—it's about being intentional. Each hat has its time and place, but only one belongs on your head at a time.

I once worked with a colleague who seemed to understand this instinctively. When she was mentoring, she was fully present, no distractions. When she was leading a strategy session, she didn't drift into small talk or side issues. She wore the hat that fit the moment, and because of that, her team always knew what to expect from her. Her clarity became their confidence.

Too many hats also lead to burnout. Every time you switch roles without intention, you drain your energy. You end up spread thin, juggling tasks that don't align with your strengths. The result is exhaustion, not excellence. Clarity isn't just a gift to your team—it's a gift to yourself. It allows you to conserve energy for the hats that truly fit.

Another trap is picking up hats that were never yours to wear in the first place. Maybe it's the finance hat when you have an accounting team, or the micromanagement hat when your team is perfectly capable. Taking on unnecessary hats doesn't show commitment; it shows mistrust. Clarity means letting others wear their own hats and trusting them to do it well.

Leadership is about identity as much as it is about responsibility. The hats you wear most often shape how people see you. If you constantly swap without intention, you'll seem scattered. But if you consistently wear the hats that align with your strengths and values, people will recognize your leadership as steady and reliable.

At the end of the day, leadership isn't about how many hats you can stack on your head—it's about knowing which one defines you best. You can own many hats, but only one or two should become your signature. Those are the hats people will remember long after the meeting ends.

So the next time you find yourself trying to juggle too many hats, pause. Ask yourself: which hat does this moment really need? Then put that one on—and put the rest away.

Reflection Journal

Which hats are you wearing right now in your leadership?

Which one feels most authentic, and which feels forced?

What hat do you need to put down this week to lead with more clarity?

[Write here]

_____

_____

_____

_____

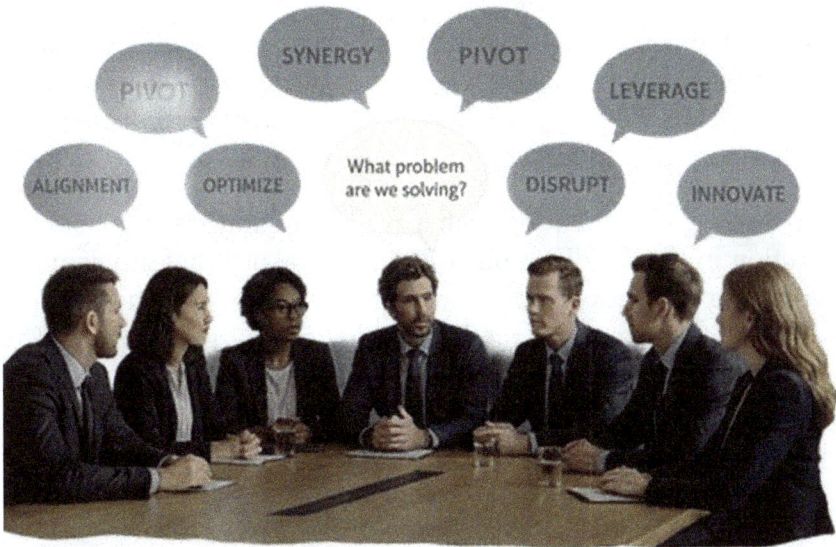

The Endless Meeting

We've all sat in one—the kind of meeting that feels like time has stopped. The agenda is vague, the purpose unclear, and the air is thick with words that sound important but mean very little. Buzzwords fly around the room like confetti: synergy, pivot, alignment, innovation. The longer it goes, the more you wonder if anyone actually knows why you're there. It's not a meeting; it's noise with a calendar invite.

I remember one meeting that stretched past two hours without a single decision being made. The conversation circled endlessly, like a carousel that nobody knew how to stop. People nodded, took notes, and offered comments, but at the end, there was no clarity about what we were actually supposed to do next. Everyone left drained, not directed.

The cost of these endless meetings is higher than most leaders realize. Time spent in noise is time stolen from action. Every unclear meeting is an hour of energy your team won't get back, an hour of momentum lost, an hour of frustration quietly building. Leaders who allow endless meetings don't just waste time—they slowly erode trust. People stop believing the meeting is worth attending because nothing ever changes when it's over.

The turning point for me came when I finally asked a simple question in the middle of one of those spirals: "What problem are we solving right now?" The room went silent. After a pause, people laughed nervously. Then, for the first time all day, the fog lifted. The noise collapsed into focus. Everyone realized we hadn't been solving a problem at all—we'd just been filling the air. From that moment, the meeting shifted. We made a decision. We left with clarity.

That question taught me something: clarity often enters through the courage to interrupt noise. Endless meetings thrive on passivity. People keep talking because nobody dares to stop the carousel. But the leader who dares to ask the right question at the right moment can bring the ride to a halt.

Noise also disguises itself as participation. Leaders sometimes mistake lots of talking for engagement. But true engagement isn't about how many people speak; it's about whether the conversation moves toward a clear outcome. Endless meetings are full of participation without progress. Clarity means shifting the goal from "Did everyone speak?" to "Did we move forward?"

One practice I adopted was to end every meeting with three questions: What did we decide? Who owns it? By when? If we couldn't answer those three questions, the meeting wasn't finished—it was just noise. That discipline didn't just shorten meetings; it built trust. People knew that if they came to a meeting I led, they'd leave knowing exactly what came next.

Clarity in meetings is a reflection of clarity in leadership. If your leadership is unfocused, your meetings will be too. But if you've done the work of finding clarity for yourself, you'll bring it into the room like oxygen. Your team will breathe easier. They'll know the meeting will have a purpose, and their time will be respected.

Endless meetings may feel like a universal law of modern work, but they're not inevitable. They exist because we allow them to. The moment you choose clarity over noise—by asking sharper questions, setting clearer goals, and respecting time—you change the culture. Meetings shift from being energy-draining to energy-giving.

The real test of a meeting isn't how long it lasts but how much clarity it creates. If people leave more confused than when they entered, you've hosted noise. If they leave with direction, ownership, and momentum, you've created signal. That's leadership.

Think back to your last meeting—did it create clarity or noise?

What's one question you can use this week to bring focus when meetings drift?

How can you model respect for people's time by leading with clarity?

[Write here]

_____

_____

_____

_____

Why Clarity Matters

Leadership without clarity is like walking along a narrow cliffside trail in the fog. Each step feels uncertain. Every turn feels dangerous. You can hear the wind and the rocks shifting below, but you can't see far enough ahead to know if the path is safe. That's what leading without clarity feels like—for you and for those who follow you. Every decision becomes heavier. Every action feels like a guess.

Clarity matters because it removes that fog. When leaders bring clarity, the path becomes visible. Suddenly, the uncertainty that once paralyzed people begins to fade. Energy that was once wasted on worry is redirected toward action. Instead of hesitating at every step, people walk with confidence because they can finally see where they're going.

I once worked on a project where the team was exhausted. Deadlines slipped, morale was low, and everyone felt like they were trudging through the dark. Meetings were filled with endless speculation: "What does leadership really want?" "Are we even on the right track?" Nobody knew, because no one had provided clarity. Then, in one meeting, a senior leader stepped in and cut through the fog. She clearly stated the goal, the boundaries, and the timeline. In less than fifteen minutes, she provided what weeks of noise hadn't. The difference was immediate. Energy returned. Decisions moved forward. Clarity turned despair into progress.

Without clarity, people burn out quickly. They spend too much energy on guessing, interpreting, and second-guessing. It's not the work itself that exhausts them—it's the fog around the work. Leaders often underestimate how much mental weight they add when they don't provide clarity. The work may be challenging, but with clarity, it feels purposeful. Without clarity, it feels pointless.

Clarity also builds trust. Teams will forgive mistakes if they know the direction is clear. They'll follow leaders through difficult seasons if they believe the path has been thought through. But when leaders shift goals weekly or hide the true objectives, trust erodes. People begin to feel like pawns in a game rather than partners in a mission. Clarity reassures them that they are not wandering aimlessly—that their work matters and is tied to something bigger.

Another reason clarity matters is efficiency. Without it, decisions get stuck in endless loops. Teams argue, projects stall, and meetings multiply because nobody can agree on the destination. With clarity, decisions come faster, because everyone is looking at the same map. Clarity eliminates wasted motion. It doesn't make the journey easy, but it makes the steps purposeful.

In my own leadership, I've seen how clarity can turn tension into unity. I once led a team that was divided over how to prioritize resources. Arguments broke out in every meeting, and resentment simmered. But when I finally sat down and clearly outlined our priorities—what we would focus on first, what would wait, and why—the arguments stopped. The same people who had been at odds became aligned, not because they suddenly agreed on everything, but because clarity gave them a shared starting point.

Clarity also fuels courage. When people can see the path, they're more willing to take risks. They're not paralyzed by the fear of the unknown. A foggy path makes people cautious; a clear one makes them bold. Leaders who provide clarity don't just make things easier—they make people braver. They unlock potential that foggy leadership keeps trapped.

In the end, clarity matters because it multiplies impact. One leader with clarity can energize an entire team. One team with clarity can shift the culture of an entire organization. The ripple effects are massive. It doesn't start with grand strategies or complicated systems. It starts with one leader deciding to turn on the light.

So ask yourself: where in your leadership are you leaving people in the fog? And where might one clear statement— one bold act of clarity—change everything for the better?

Where in your leadership do you feel like you're walking in fog?

What single act of clarity could lift that fog for your team or family?

How might clarity unlock courage in those you lead this week?

[Write here]

———————————————————————————

———————————————————————————

———————————————————————————

———————————————————————————

The Cost of Noise

Noise always comes with a price. On the surface, it feels harmless—just more chatter, another email, one more meeting. But underneath, noise quietly drains the very things leaders and teams need most: time, energy, and focus. Left unchecked, the cost of noise becomes enormous, even though most organizations never stop to calculate it.

The first cost is time. Every moment spent sorting through unclear instructions or sitting in a meeting without purpose is time stolen from meaningful work. I once joined a project that held daily two-hour update calls. The intention was accountability, but the result was exhaustion. By the end of the week, nearly a full day had been lost to noise. When we finally cut the updates down to thirty minutes, productivity skyrocketed—not because people suddenly worked harder, but because they were freed from unnecessary noise.

The second cost is energy. Noise doesn't just waste hours; it drains people emotionally. Confusion creates frustration, and frustration burns energy faster than effort ever could. It's the difference between rowing against the current and rowing with it. The work may look the same on the outside, but one leaves you depleted while the other fuels momentum.

Noise also has a cost in morale. Teams that live in constant noise start to feel undervalued. When people can't see the purpose in their work, motivation fades. I've seen brilliant employees lose passion because they were caught in a fog of shifting goals and unclear communication. They weren't burned out from working too hard— they were burned out from working without clarity.

There's also the cost of opportunity. While leaders are distracted by noise, they miss the signals that matter. Noise drowns out the weak but important signals—the early warnings, the new opportunities, the quiet voices with brilliant ideas. By the time leaders notice what they missed, it's often too late.

I once heard a mentor describe it this way: "Noise is like trying to listen to a symphony with static in your headphones." The music is still there, but you can't appreciate its beauty. Opportunities are still present, but they're buried beneath distortion. Clarity is the act of turning down the static so the real music can be heard.

Noise also corrodes trust. When leaders constantly change direction without explaining why, or when they communicate in ways that confuse more than clarify, people lose confidence. They begin to believe that leadership doesn't know what it's doing—or worse, doesn't care enough to provide clarity. Trust, once lost, is difficult to rebuild.

The financial cost of noise is real, too. Studies show that unclear communication and wasted meetings cost organizations billions annually. But beyond the dollars, the hidden cost is momentum. Teams stuck in noise move slower, innovate less, and accomplish less than they are capable of.

The good news is that noise is not inevitable. Leaders can reduce its cost by making clarity a discipline. Every clear decision, every concise message, every purposeful meeting pays dividends. The cost of clarity may feel high in the moment—it requires time, thought, and sometimes hard conversations—but the return is exponential.

In the end, the real question isn't whether noise has a cost. The question is whether you're willing to keep paying it. Leaders who choose clarity may work harder upfront, but they save themselves and their teams from years of wasted effort, frustration, and lost opportunities. That is the true economy of leadership.

Where do you see noise costing your team the most right now—time, energy, morale, or opportunity?

What is one change you can make this week to reduce the static and restore clarity?

How can you measure the "cost of noise" in your own leadership?

[Write here]

_____

_____

_____

_____

Small Steps Create Signal

When leaders think about clarity, they often imagine grand speeches, sweeping visions, or bold decisions that reshape an organization overnight. But in reality, clarity is rarely born in big moments. More often, it emerges through small, consistent steps taken day after day. These steps may look ordinary, even insignificant, but over time they create a powerful signal that cuts through the noise.

I once worked with a leader who began every meeting by restating the purpose in one clear sentence. At first, it felt repetitive. But slowly, I realized what she was doing—she was training us to listen for the signal. Over weeks and months, that simple habit aligned the entire team. People stopped drifting off into side conversations or irrelevant updates because they always knew what the meeting was about. One small step, repeated with discipline, created clarity.

Small steps matter because they compound. Just like static disappears when you carefully fine-tune a radio dial, clarity emerges when leaders make small adjustments every day. A quick check-in with a teammate. A concise email that focuses on one key message instead of ten. A moment to ask, "What problem are we solving right now?" None of these steps feels dramatic, but together, they amplify the signal.

The danger is that leaders often underestimate these small steps. We convince ourselves that clarity must be complicated, that it takes a new system, a big reorganization, or a groundbreaking strategy. But some of the most effective clarity comes from leaders who are willing to take the small, consistent actions others ignore.

Think about how trust is built. It's not one grand gesture that earns loyalty—it's a thousand small moments of honesty, consistency, and presence. Clarity works the same way. People don't believe you because of a single inspiring moment; they believe you because your signal comes through the same, day after day.

I remember a season when my own leadership felt shaky. Projects were stalling, and I worried my team had lost faith. Instead of trying to make a big, dramatic change, I chose one small step: I ended every email with the same line, "Here's the one thing that matters this week." At first, it felt almost silly. But within a month, I noticed a shift. My team began echoing that line back to me in updates. They had tuned into the signal.

Small steps also make clarity accessible. Not every leader has the authority to deliver sweeping change, but every leader can choose one act of clarity today. Whether it's a team lead clarifying the day's priorities or a parent reminding their family of what matters most this week, small steps are available to everyone.

And here's the beauty: small steps are sustainable. Big changes often create burnout because they require massive effort. Small steps, repeated consistently, create rhythm. Over time, that rhythm builds culture. A culture shaped by clarity doesn't need to be reminded of what matters—it lives it out naturally.

Clarity doesn't arrive all at once like a lightning bolt. It builds slowly, like a lighthouse beam sweeping across the water, growing stronger with every rotation. Leaders who embrace the power of small steps discover that they don't need to shout to be heard. Their signal grows clearer because they've built it, day by day, with intentional action.

So don't underestimate the small steps. They may not trend on social media. They may not make headlines. But they are the quiet, steady rhythm that turns noise into signal and followers into leaders.

What small step can you take today to amplify clarity for your team or family?

How might repeating one act of clarity create momentum over time?

What rhythm of small steps could you commit to this month?

[Write here]

_____

_____

_____

_____

Stories of Small Starts

Every great movement, every lasting legacy, begins with a small start. Yet when we look back at successful leaders, businesses, or families, we often forget how humble their beginnings really were. We see the polished results and assume they must have begun with the same clarity and confidence they now display. The truth is, clarity usually begins with one small step—a seed planted long before the tree became visible.

I once met a nonprofit leader whose organization now spans multiple countries. When I asked her how it started, she smiled and told me it began with her offering sandwiches to two kids in her neighborhood. She didn't have a five-year plan or a global vision at the time. She just saw two hungry children and decided to do something about it. That small start, repeated and refined over years, became a movement.

The same pattern shows up in business. Many of the world's most recognizable companies began in garages, basements, or dorm rooms. Their founders didn't start with a billion-dollar enterprise. They started with one product, one customer, one problem to solve. Clarity didn't come from the grandness of the vision; it came from taking the first step and learning along the way.

Small starts matter because they teach humility. They remind us that leadership isn't about arriving fully formed—it's about being willing to begin even when the picture is incomplete. Leaders who wait for perfect conditions before starting rarely start at all. Those who take imperfect action create momentum that builds clarity over time.

I've seen this in families too. Parents sometimes feel overwhelmed by the enormity of raising children, worrying about the big picture of education, career, or future success. But clarity in family leadership often begins with the smallest starts—consistent bedtime routines, regular conversations at the dinner table, or simply showing up at the school play. Those small acts of presence, repeated over years, form the foundation of trust and direction.

One of the most inspiring leaders I knew used to say, "Don't despise small beginnings." He understood that small starts carry hidden power. They don't look impressive at first, but they contain the seeds of future greatness. Every oak tree was once an acorn. Every lighthouse beam begins as a single spark.

The challenge is that small starts are easy to dismiss. They don't attract attention. They don't generate applause. But clarity doesn't need to be flashy. It needs to be real. When you embrace the discipline of small starts, you align yourself with the way growth truly happens—incrementally, steadily, quietly.

What matters most isn't how big your start looks, but whether it's rooted in clarity. A small start built on noise won't last. A small start built on clarity—on knowing who you are and what problem you're solving—becomes the kind of foundation that can hold extraordinary weight in the future.

Leaders who embrace small starts also inspire others. When people see you willing to begin without waiting for perfection, they feel empowered to do the same. Your courage to take a small step gives others permission to step forward too. That's how movements begin—not with one giant leap, but with many small starts that join together into something larger than any one person could imagine.

So the next time you feel overwhelmed by the enormity of your goals, remember: clarity doesn't demand that you see the whole staircase. It only asks that you take the first step. That small start, if rooted in clarity, will carry you farther than you ever thought possible.

Reflection Journal

What small start have you been overlooking because it felt too insignificant?

How might that small step create momentum toward greater clarity?

Who could benefit if you stopped waiting for perfection and started today?

[Write here]

_____

_____

_____

_____

Becoming a Lighthouse

A lighthouse doesn't chase ships. It doesn't shout across the waves, run up and down the shore, or try to impress with fireworks. It stands steady, anchored to the rocks, shining its light for anyone who needs direction. That's what clarity in leadership looks like— less noise, more presence. Leaders who become lighthouses don't chase attention; they provide direction.

Early in my career, I thought leadership meant being everywhere at once. I ran from meeting to meeting, answered every email within minutes, and tried to personally solve every problem. I was exhausted—and worse, my team was still unclear. My busyness created noise, not clarity. It wasn't until a mentor told me, "Stop trying to be the boat. Be the lighthouse," that I understood. My job wasn't to run around proving my value—it was to stand steady, shining a clear signal others could count on.

Lighthouses are reliable. Sailors trust them because they know the light will always be there. Leaders who embody clarity build the same kind of trust. When your team knows what you stand for, what you value, and how you'll respond in difficult times, they begin to relax. They stop second-guessing your motives or worrying about hidden agendas. Like sailors scanning the coast, they can navigate safely because your light is steady.

The power of the lighthouse isn't in its noise but in its consistency. A single flash of brilliance won't guide a ship through a storm. It takes steady, repeated beams. In the same way, clarity isn't proven in one big speech—it's proven in the day-to-day consistency of your words and actions.

I once worked under a leader who embodied this. No matter how chaotic things became, she never raised her voice, never panicked, and never contradicted herself. Her clarity was like a beam across rough seas. Even when the outcome was uncertain, we trusted her because she never wavered. She didn't try to be spectacular; she chose to be steady.

Becoming a lighthouse also means accepting that not everyone will listen. Some ships will ignore the light and crash anyway. Some will sail by without noticing. That's not failure. Your role is not to control every outcome; your role is to shine consistently for those who are looking for direction. Leadership clarity doesn't guarantee results, but it guarantees you've done your part.

It also means being willing to shine even when storms rage. Clarity matters most when conditions are worst. In times of calm, almost anyone can lead. But in the fog, in the storm, in the chaos—that's when the light of clarity becomes priceless. Leaders who stand steady in the storm are the ones people remember forever.

The metaphor of the lighthouse reminds us that clarity is more about being than doing. It's about the kind of presence you bring into every room, every conversation, every decision. Do people feel steadier because you are there? Do they leave with more clarity than they had before? If so, you are becoming a lighthouse.

And here's the paradox: lighthouses don't move, but they create movement. They stand still, yet they save countless lives. Leaders who embody clarity may seem quiet, but their influence ripples far beyond what they can see. That's the kind of impact noise can never achieve.

So ask yourself: are you trying to be the boat, darting from wave to wave? Or are you becoming the lighthouse—anchored, steady, and shining a light others can depend on? The difference isn't just about style; it's about legacy.

Where in your leadership are you chasing attention instead of shining steadily?

What would it look like for you to become a lighthouse for your team or family?

How might consistency—not noise—become your greatest source of influence?

[Write here]

_____

_____

_____

_____

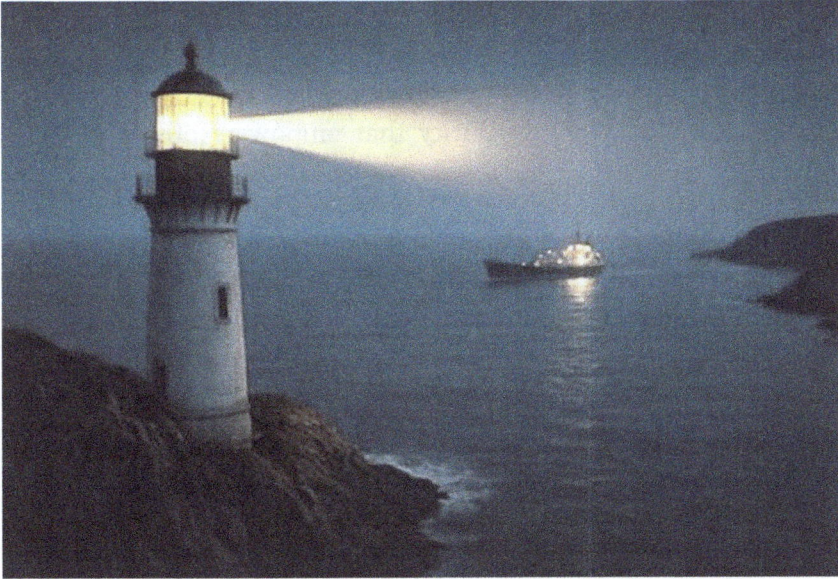

Closing Thought

As we come to the end of this Introduction, I want to leave you with one final picture of clarity. Imagine standing on a shoreline at dusk. The waves are restless, the sky is fading, and the air is thick with noise from gulls, surf, and wind. Then, just beyond the horizon, a single light appears. It doesn't erase the noise, but it gives you a direction. That is what clarity does. It doesn't eliminate every challenge; it simply provides a way forward.

Leadership in today's world can feel overwhelming. The noise is louder than ever—social media voices, endless advice, shifting expectations, and constant pressure to do more. It's tempting to believe you need to match the volume, to out-shout the noise with more noise of your own. But that's a losing game. Clarity is never about being the loudest; it's about being the most consistent.

Think of the leaders you admire most. Chances are, it isn't their flashy speeches or clever slogans that stuck with you. It's the way they helped you see something more clearly. It's how they gave you confidence when things felt uncertain. It's how their words and actions aligned so well that you trusted their direction. That's the true mark of leadership—clarity that empowers others to move forward.

I once asked a friend what made her trust her manager during a difficult season. She said, "He didn't always have the answers, but he always made the next step clear." That line has stayed with me. Leadership isn't about having every answer; it's about giving people the clarity they need for the step they must take today. Tomorrow will bring its own challenges. But if you can bring clarity to this moment, you've done something powerful.

Clarity also matters because it multiplies. When one leader models clarity, it spreads to others. Teams begin to speak more clearly, meetings become more purposeful, families feel steadier. Over time, clarity becomes culture. And culture is what endures long after individuals move on.

Noise, on the other hand, always fades. Today's buzzword will be forgotten tomorrow. The guru parade will move on to the next trend. But clarity lasts. It's remembered because it makes a difference. It transforms noise into meaning, chaos into focus, hesitation into courage.

Closing this Introduction doesn't mean the journey ends. It means you've taken the first step. The pages ahead are designed to help you build clarity in your own leadership—whether in business, in your community, or in your family. Each part of this book will challenge you to practice clarity, not just admire it.

And here's the truth: you already have everything you need to begin. Clarity isn't found in a hidden formula or a secret guru's toolkit. It's built by slowing down, asking better questions, and committing to small, consistent steps. Every leader—whether leading a company, a classroom, or a dinner table—has the capacity to become a lighthouse for others.

So as you step into the rest of this book, ask yourself one question: What would it look like for me to lead with clarity today? Not tomorrow, not next year, but today. Because clarity is not something you wait for. It's something you practice.

What is one area of your life where clarity is most needed right now?

How can you begin practicing clarity today, even in small steps?

Who in your world might need your lighthouse beam this week?

[Write here]

_____

_____

_____

_____

The Journey Ahead: Your Roadmap to Clarity

This playbook is designed as a journey. Each Part builds on the last, moving you from understanding clarity, to practicing it daily, to applying it in bigger ways. Think of it as climbing a mountain—each stage takes you higher, with the summit in sight.

Part I – The 30-Day Clarity Playbook

You'll begin with a practical, daily journey. Each day includes a story, an activity, and space for reflection. These 30 days will help you cut through noise, practice clarity in small steps, and build habits that anchor you as a leader.

Part II – Deepening the Practice

Next, you'll learn how to apply clarity in more complex situations. Through expanded lessons and case studies, you'll discover how clarity transforms not just your personal habits, but also how teams and organizations operate.

Part III – Applying Clarity to Life & Leadership

Here we move beyond practice into real-world application. You'll explore how to bring clarity into your business leadership, your role in your community, and even your family life. Clarity is not confined to one space—it's a way of living.

Part I – The 30-Day Clarity Playbook

Day 1: Identity (Zone of Genius)

There's a moment in every leader's journey when they realize they've been chasing other people's definitions of success. Day 1 is about pressing pause on that chase. I remember sitting in a meeting years ago, surrounded by colleagues who seemed so sure of themselves. I kept measuring my worth against their titles, their confidence, their polished stories. But something shifted when I asked myself, quietly, 'What is it that I do differently? What do I bring that nobody else can?' That single question planted a seed.

At first, the question felt unsettling. I didn't have an answer, and not having an answer made me uncomfortable. But clarity rarely arrives fully formed. It begins as a whisper, a subtle nudge that says, 'Look closer.' That whisper stayed with me for days, then weeks. Slowly, I began to notice the things people sought me out for, the small moments where I made a difference without realizing it.

It wasn't about being the loudest in the room. My contribution showed up in quieter ways-listening when others talked over each other, translating complexity into something manageable, making people feel like they belonged. I had dismissed these moments as insignificant, but they were actually glimpses of my genius.

The truth is, we often overlook our greatest strengths because they feel natural to us. We assume that if something is easy for us, it must be easy for everyone. But ease is a clue, not a dismissal. Your genius hides in the places where effort feels light, where you almost lose track of time because you're so absorbed in the work.

On Day 1, your job is not to define your genius in perfect terms. It's simply to notice. Notice when people light up after talking with you. Notice when you solve something without breaking a sweat. These moments matter because they're not coincidences-they're patterns worth paying attention to.

The story of Day 1 is this: you already carry a zone of genius inside you. The work is not to create it, but to uncover it. And the first step in uncovering it is paying attention to the sparks you've been ignoring.

Activity: Write down three moments in the past month when you felt fully alive or energized. Don't overthink it. These are likely windows into your genius.

Reflection: What patterns do you notice in those moments? Do they point to skills, perspectives, or values that set you apart?

Day 2: Identity (Zone of Genius)

On Day 2, we lean into curiosity. I once worked with a colleague who seemed to thrive in chaos. Deadlines didn't rattle her. Confusion energized her. At first, I thought her genius was simply stress tolerance. But as I watched more closely, I realized it wasn't about stress at all. Her gift was creating calm. In the middle of stormy projects, she was the steady voice that helped everyone else breathe.

Her presence showed me something important: our genius often hides in the ordinary. What she considered 'just being herself' was actually a rare skill. Others leaned on her because they trusted her steadiness. To her, it was effortless. To them, it was life-saving. That's how genius works-it feels ordinary to you, but extraordinary to others.

Think about the moments when people thank you for something you barely noticed doing. Maybe it was a quick piece of advice, a gesture of kindness, or a problem you solved without breaking a sweat. Those aren't accidents. They're breadcrumbs pointing you toward your genius.

We dismiss these moments because they don't feel grand. We assume genius has to look flashy or dramatic. But the truth is, most genius is quiet. It shows up in the way you listen, the way you notice details others miss, the way you connect people or ideas that don't seem connected.

Day 2 is about noticing the effortless. Your genius lives in the spaces where you feel like you're 'just being yourself.' The more you pay attention, the more you'll realize those effortless acts are anything but common.

The story of Day 2 is this: your genius isn't hiding. It's simply waiting for you to take it seriously. Today is about learning to honor the effortless as evidence of your brilliance.

Activity: Ask two people you trust to describe a time when you made their life easier, better, or clearer. Write down their answers without judgment.

Reflection: What surprised you about their perspective? Did they notice strengths you've been taking for granted?

Day 3: Identity (Zone of Genius)

Day 3 is about contrast. Sometimes the fastest way to discover your genius is to look at what drains you. I once worked in a role that demanded endless data entry. Every day felt like wading through mud. I was capable, but never energized. Contrast that with the moments I got to explain the bigger picture to my team. I left those conversations buzzing with energy.

The difference was striking. The same job that drained me also gave me life in specific situations. That contrast became the lens through which I saw myself more clearly. I realized that while I could survive in tasks that felt mechanical, I thrived in moments of translation-taking something complex and making it simple for others.

We often ignore frustration, treating it as something to push through. But frustration is a teacher. It tells us what environments and tasks dull our light. When paired with noticing the moments that energize us, it becomes a powerful tool for clarity.

Think of it this way: the tasks that drain you aren't just inconveniences. They're clues. They highlight where you don't belong, which in turn makes it easier to see where you do. The contrast between what drains and what energizes is often sharper than we realize.

Day 3 invites you to use frustration as fuel. Instead of resenting the draining tasks, let them point you toward the places where your genius can shine. The more you honor the contrast, the clearer the map of your genius becomes.

The story of Day 3 is about honoring contrast. Discomfort isn't wasted-it's a signpost. Pay attention to it, and it will guide you toward the work you were made to do.

Activity: List three tasks that drain you and three that energize you. Circle the energizers and ask: how can I spend more time here?

Reflection: What does the contrast reveal about your genius? Where is your energy trying to guide you?

Day 4: Identity (Zone of Genius)

On Day 4, we talk about childhood clues. As kids, we often show sparks of genius before the world teaches us to fit in. I loved taking apart radios just to see how they worked. I wasn't trying to become an engineer-I was just endlessly curious about systems. That curiosity grew into a lifelong habit of simplifying complexity.

Think back to what you loved doing before someone told you to be practical. Did you line up your toys? Tell elaborate stories? Organize your friends into games? These aren't just memories. They're breadcrumbs from your earliest genius.

One client I worked with realized her genius by revisiting childhood play. As a kid, she organized elaborate pretend businesses with her friends. As an adult, she became a systems architect. The connection wasn't random-her childhood instincts had been pointing her in that direction all along.

The world often teaches us to downplay those instincts. We're told to grow up, focus on the serious stuff. But the truth is, our childlike patterns never disappear. They wait for us to rediscover them as adults.

Day 4 is about reclaiming those sparks. You don't need to recreate your childhood exactly-you just need to notice what your early passions reveal about your wiring. Chances are, those sparks are still alive, waiting to be rekindled.

The story of Day 4 is this: your genius leaves clues early. Pay attention to them. Childhood passions are not random-they are signals, and they're worth listening to again.

Activity: Write about one thing you loved doing as a child that still brings you joy today. How does it connect to your current work or aspirations?

Reflection: What childhood sparks are worth reigniting? How might they shape your zone of genius today?

Day 5: Identity (Zone of Genius)

Day 5 is about owning your genius. By now, you've gathered clues-from your effortless strengths, your contrasts, and your childhood sparks. But genius doesn't serve anyone if it stays hidden. It needs to be named, claimed, and shared.

I remember the first time I said out loud, 'I simplify complexity so people can focus on what matters.' It felt small at first, almost too simple. But the more I shared it, the more people nodded. They understood me. And in that understanding, doors opened.

Naming your genius is an act of courage. It means risking vulnerability, risking the possibility that others may not understand. But without naming it, clarity remains locked inside. When you speak it, you invite others to recognize it too.

One leader I coached resisted naming her genius for months. She feared it would sound arrogant. But when she finally declared, 'I create order out of chaos,' her team celebrated her. They had seen it all along-they just needed her to claim it.

Day 5 is about courage. It's about putting words to what has been quietly shaping your life. The sentence doesn't need to be perfect; it just needs to be honest. Perfection can come later. Clarity grows with use.

The story of Day 5 is this: clarity without courage remains unused potential. Courage turns clarity into action. Today is about taking that step.

Activity: Draft one simple sentence that describes your genius. Begin with: 'I... so that...' Don't worry about perfection-just start.

Reflection: How does it feel to put words to your genius? What shifts when you say it out loud?

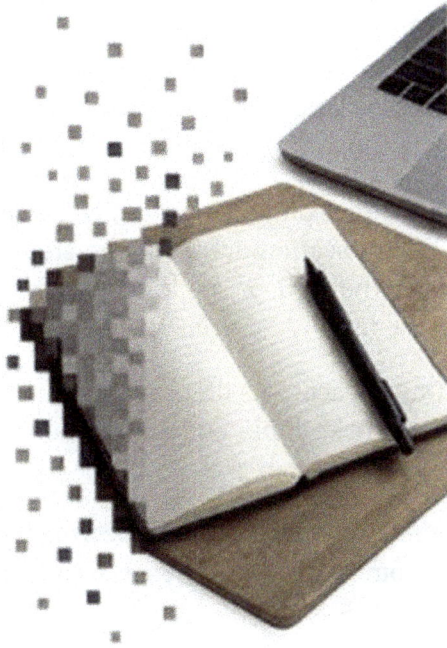

Day 6: Environment (Workspace & Energy)

Day 6 is about environment. I once visited a colleague's office and was struck by the difference between us. Her desk was spotless, her calendar color-coded, her whiteboard filled with neatly outlined goals. Walking into her space felt like breathing fresh air. Then I returned to my own desk, stacked with papers, sticky notes, and coffee mugs, and I felt the weight of clutter pressing in on me.

It wasn't that I was less capable, but my environment made me feel scattered. I realized then that clarity isn't just about the mind-it's about the spaces that hold our thoughts. An environment in chaos multiplies chaos in the mind. An environment in order makes room for clearer thinking and stronger energy.

This doesn't mean we all need minimalist desks or pristine offices. What it means is that our environment should reflect the clarity we want to cultivate. For some, that's a creative mess that sparks ideas. For others, it's clean lines and open surfaces. The key is intentionality-choosing rather than drifting.

Your environment speaks back to you every day. It whispers either, 'You're scattered,' or 'You're steady.' If you've been feeling foggy, overwhelmed, or stuck, start by listening to what your environment is saying.

Day 6 teaches us that clarity isn't only internal. It's external. Where you work, think, and live influences how your genius shows up in the world.

The story of Day 6 is this: when your environment is aligned, it becomes an ally. When it's cluttered, it becomes resistance. The choice is yours.

Activity: Choose one small area of your environment-your desk, your inbox, or your calendar-and bring order to it today.

Reflection: How did this small act of order shift your energy? What clarity did you feel afterward?

Day 7: Environment (Workspace & Energy)

Day 7 reminds us that environment isn't just physical—it's digital too. A friend once admitted that her computer desktop had over 200 icons. Every time she opened it, she felt overwhelmed before she even began her day. It wasn't her workload that stressed her, it was the noise of digital clutter.

We underestimate how much our digital spaces shape us. Notifications that ping endlessly, tabs that pile up, emails that flood our inbox—each one is a small demand, a thief of attention. Over time, these small thieves add up to exhaustion.

When I helped her clear her desktop, archive files, and create a clean folder system, she told me it felt like losing 20 pounds of invisible weight. Nothing in her workload changed, but her mind felt lighter because her digital environment finally matched the clarity she was chasing.

But it doesn't stop at screens. Look around your physical workspace. The piles of papers on your desk, the half-finished projects stacked in the corner, the sticky notes with reminders you no longer notice—each one whispers to your brain, "You still haven't dealt with me." These whispers pile up until your body feels as heavy as your inbox. A clear desk is more than aesthetics—it's a stage where focus has room to perform.

Clutter has a way of becoming background noise that you stop noticing consciously, but your subconscious never stops registering it. That's why walking into a messy room can feel draining even if you aren't actively thinking about it. Your brain is quietly spending energy tracking all those loose ends. When you clear the clutter, you also clear the invisible mental tabs running in the background.

The same principle applies to relationships. Your environment isn't just made of objects—it's shaped by people. Spend a week around constant complainers, and your energy will sag. Spend the same week around people who are building, creating, and encouraging, and you'll feel lifted. Attention thrives in environments where energy is protected, not depleted.

And don't overlook your sensory environment. Lighting, noise, even the chair you sit in—all of these send signals to your body about how safe and focused you can be. A poorly lit room can make you feel sluggish; constant background noise can keep your nervous system on alert. Small tweaks like adjusting your lighting or adding a plant can shift your energy more than you realize.

Day 7 is an invitation to become intentional about every layer of environment—digital, physical, relational, and sensory. Each one either supports or sabotages clarity. Stewardship here doesn't mean perfection; it means designing spaces that quietly tell your mind, "You're safe to focus."

Day 7 is about stewardship—not just of your time, but of your attention. Attention is your most valuable resource, and your environment is either guarding it or leaking it away.

The story of Day 7 is this: when you choose clarity in the unseen spaces, you reclaim energy for the work that matters most.

Activity: Clear your digital workspace today. Close unused tabs, archive old files, and turn off one unnecessary notification. Then, take five minutes to clear one small corner of your physical space—a drawer, a shelf, or even your desk surface.

Reflection: How does your focus shift when your environment mirrors clarity? Who in your environment gives you energy, and who drains it?

Day 8: Environment (Workspace & Energy)

On Day 8, we explore routines. A client once told me she felt scattered every morning until she built a simple ritual: ten minutes of journaling with her coffee. That rhythm became the anchor of her day, giving her focus and calm before emails and meetings demanded her attention.

Routines aren't glamorous. They rarely make headlines. But they create a scaffolding for your genius to show up consistently. When you start your day with intention, you step into clarity before chaos can grab hold.

I learned this myself when I shifted from rolling out of bed and diving into work to starting my mornings with a walk and a short plan for the day. The difference wasn't small—it was transformational. My mornings went from reaction to creation.

Your environment isn't just a space; it's also a pattern. A routine shapes the emotional climate of your day. It tells your mind: here's how we begin, here's how we sustain, here's how we close.

I've also noticed that routines don't just serve individuals—they shape culture. A team that begins meetings with five minutes of gratitude will carry a different energy than a team that jumps straight into problems. A family that eats together each evening builds a rhythm of connection that outlasts the busyness of schedules. Routines quietly communicate what matters most.

What makes routines powerful is not their complexity, but their consistency. A two-hour morning ritual might collapse under pressure, but a two-minute ritual—like writing down one intention or taking three deep breaths—can survive even the busiest day. Small routines that are sustainable matter more than elaborate ones that can't hold up over time.

Routines also anchor you in uncertain times. When life feels unstable—whether due to work stress, family changes, or global events—the simple act of keeping one rhythm reminds your mind and body that not everything is shifting. That stability gives you a foothold to face challenges with clarity.

There's also a relational ripple effect. When your routine brings calm into your life, you carry that calm into every interaction. Colleagues notice. Family feels it. Even strangers respond differently when you show up grounded. In this way, your private ritual becomes public leadership, radiating steadiness without a word.

And don't forget endings. Morning routines get the spotlight, but closing routines matter just as much. A short reflection at the end of the day, turning off screens before bed, or even noting one win from the day creates closure. Without it, your mind drags unfinished energy into tomorrow. With it, you step into rest with clarity.

Finally, routines are not about perfection. Missing a day doesn't erase the habit; it simply invites you to return. Think of them like music—if you miss a beat, the rhythm continues. What matters is rejoining the song. That's how rituals become resilient, not rigid.

And here's the surprising part: routines actually make you freer. People sometimes resist them, fearing they'll feel restricted. But in reality, routines remove decision fatigue. By automating the basics, you conserve energy for the creative, meaningful choices. Clarity thrives not because every moment is rigidly planned, but because the important moments aren't wasted on chaos.

Day 8 is about rhythm. Clarity doesn't happen by accident—it is cultivated through the habits we choose. When you establish rhythms that align with clarity, you don't just have better days— you build a better life.

The story of Day 8 is this: clarity is a practice, not an event. Rituals are how we practice it daily.

Activity: Design one intentional ritual for your day—a short walk, journaling, or planning session—and practice it tomorrow.

Reflection: How does a small ritual set the tone for your clarity and energy?

Day 9: Environment (Workspace & Energy)

Day 9 asks us to notice energy leaks. I remember a season when I said yes to every meeting invite. By noon, I was drained, not because I lacked energy, but because my environment was crowded with interruptions.

One week, I decided to experiment. I blocked out one hour each morning as "no meeting" time. At first, colleagues pushed back. But then something remarkable happened: my productivity doubled, and my stress dropped. The problem wasn't my capacity. It was my boundaries.

Environments are shaped not only by things but by permissions. When you allow everything and everyone to invade your time, you dilute your genius. Boundaries are the invisible walls that protect clarity.

Think of boundaries as the architecture of your energy. They don't lock you in—they keep distractions out. Every boundary you create is an act of respect for your clarity and your future self.

I've seen entire teams transform when they establish boundaries together. One group I worked with created "focus afternoons" twice a week—no emails, no meetings, just deep work. At first, it felt radical, but soon they noticed fewer errors, faster turnaround, and higher morale. Boundaries didn't just protect individual clarity—they elevated collective performance.

Here's the paradox: the more successful you become, the more your boundaries will be tested. People assume access to your time is unlimited, but the higher your impact, the more precious each hour becomes. Without strong boundaries, growth becomes unsustainable. Clarity demands the courage to guard your calendar like the asset it is.

Boundaries also teach others how to treat you. Every yes and no is a signal about what you value. If you answer emails at midnight, people will expect it. If you always say yes to last-minute requests, you train others to bypass your priorities. Boundaries aren't just for you—they are silent lessons in leadership.

And it's not only about meetings or messages. Boundaries extend to your mental space. Worrying about things outside your control, replaying old mistakes, or letting negative voices live rent-free in your head are forms of permission, too. Guarding your energy means choosing what you dwell on as carefully as what you put on your calendar.

Physical space matters here as well. A door you close, a phone you silence, or a workspace you protect sends a clear signal: this time is dedicated. Small cues reinforce big commitments. When you design your environment to support boundaries, you make it easier to keep them.

Finally, remember that boundaries grow stronger with practice. The first "no" may feel heavy, but over time, it becomes natural. Each time you reinforce a boundary, you reclaim a piece of your energy. Over weeks and months, those reclaimed pieces build a reservoir of clarity you can draw on for your best work.

And here's the truth: boundaries aren't about saying no to others as much as they're about saying yes to what matters most. When you guard your best hours, you're giving yourself permission to bring your highest energy to your most important work. That's not selfish—it's stewardship.

Day 9 is about reclaiming ownership. Too often, we act like guests in our own environments, waiting for others to set the terms. But clarity comes when you declare, "This is how I work best," and then protect that space.

The story of Day 9 is this: boundaries don't limit clarity—they protect it. And when you guard your energy, you amplify your genius.

Activity: Look at your calendar for the week. Decline or reschedule one meeting or commitment that doesn't align with your clarity.

Reflection: How does setting one boundary today shift your sense of control and focus? Day 10: Environment (Workspace & Energy)

On Day 10, we integrate. Over the past days, you've noticed the power of space, digital order, routines, and boundaries. Together, these pieces create an environment where clarity can grow.

Think of it like tending a garden. No single act-pulling weeds, watering, planting seeds-creates growth on its own. But together, they create conditions where growth becomes inevitable. Your genius needs the same: conditions that make it easier to show up fully.

A leader I coached once told me he thought clarity was about waiting for inspiration. But as we worked, he realized inspiration was a byproduct of alignment. When his environment, routines, and boundaries lined up, he didn't need to wait for inspiration-it found him.

Clarity isn't about perfection. It's about alignment. Alignment doesn't mean everything is flawless; it means everything is moving in the same direction.

Day 10 invites you to step back and see the bigger picture. Your environment is no longer just where you live or work-it has become a mirror of who you are becoming.

The story of Day 10 is this: when your environment reflects your values, clarity becomes natural instead of forced. You stop fighting your surroundings and start being supported by them.

Activity: Write down three changes you've made in your environment over the past five days. Commit to maintaining them for the next month.

Reflection: How does an aligned environment empower your genius and clarity?

Reflection Journal

What is one area of your life where clarity is most needed right now?

How can you begin practicing clarity today, even in small steps?

Who in your world might need your lighthouse beam this week?

[Write here]

_____

_____

_____

_____

Day 11: Narrative (Personal Story & Messaging)

Day 11 is about the hidden stories we carry inside ourselves. Early in my career, I clung to the label of 'not ready.' Every opportunity felt like something I wasn't yet qualified for, even though my results told a different story. Looking back, I see how that inner narrative held me back more than any lack of skill ever did.

Our self-talk becomes a script, and that script can quietly guide our decisions. When the story in your head is 'I'm not ready,' you hesitate. You shrink. You stay small. And people begin to accept the smaller version of you, not because it's who you are, but because it's the version you've allowed them to see.

I've worked with people who carried different versions of this story- 'I'm not creative,' 'I'm not a leader,' 'I'm not enough.' None of these were true, but the repetition gave them power. Stories don't need to be true to shape us-they only need to be believed.

The turning point came when I caught myself repeating that story one too many times. I wrote it down and stared at the words: 'I'm not ready.' Seeing it on paper stripped it of its mystery. It was just a sentence, not a fact. And if I could write it, I could also rewrite it.

This is where clarity begins: by noticing the story already running in your head. You cannot change what you won't acknowledge. Awareness is the first act of authorship. Once you name it, you can decide whether it deserves to remain part of your story.

The story of Day 11 is this: you are the author of your own narrative. Limiting stories only stay powerful if you keep telling them. Today is about noticing the script-and beginning to take back the pen.

Activity: Write down one phrase you often tell yourself. Ask: does this story empower me, or does it limit me?

Reflection: What happens when you challenge a limiting story by writing a new one in its place?

Day 12: Narrative (Personal Story & Messaging)

On Day 12, we look at reframing the past. A friend once told me she regretted years spent in a job she hated. 'I wasted so much time,' she said. But as we unpacked her story, she realized those years had taught her patience, resilience, and the ability to lead under pressure. Her story wasn't wasted time-it was training.

We all carry chapters of our story that we wish we could erase. Seasons of frustration, failure, or seeming stagnation. It's easy to dismiss those chapters as wasted. But the truth is, they hold clues to your genius just as much as the highlight reel does.

Think of your past as raw material. The pain, the failures, the missteps-they are not weights meant to hold you down. They are bricks, waiting to be arranged into a foundation. How you frame them determines whether they keep you stuck or give you strength.

I've coached leaders who thought they had nothing valuable to share because their careers weren't linear. Yet those zig-zags were the very thing that gave them perspective others didn't have. The detours made their insights richer, their empathy deeper, their leadership more human.

Reframing the past doesn't mean pretending it was all good. It means asking, 'What did this season give me that I can use now?' Every chapter leaves behind a resource if you're willing to see it that way.

The story of Day 12 is this: your past is not a burden, it's a toolbox. The power of your story lies not in what happened, but in how you choose to frame it now.

Activity: Choose one difficult season of your life. Write about it as if it was training for the clarity you're stepping into today.

Reflection: How does reframing your past shift your sense of possibility for the future?

Day 13: Narrative (Personal Story & Messaging)

Day 13 is about voice. I once worked with a leader who was brilliant, but his words built walls instead of bridges. He spoke in jargon, layering complexity into every sentence. People nodded politely in meetings, but nobody left inspired. His message died in the delivery.

Then he began experimenting with stories. Instead of quoting frameworks, he shared how he learned lessons from his childhood or how a mistake became a turning point. Suddenly, people leaned in. They remembered his points. His voice became an invitation instead of a lecture.

Your voice is more than the words you choose-it's the courage to speak plainly in a world addicted to complexity. It's the decision to connect instead of impress. When you tell a story instead of listing a fact, you create a bridge that others want to cross.

I've seen leaders transform entire teams simply by shifting their language. They went from issuing instructions to sharing stories, and the difference was night and day. People stopped obeying and started believing.

The truth is, your authentic voice doesn't need polishing-it needs practice. The more you use it, the clearer and stronger it becomes. Don't wait for perfect phrasing. Speak honestly and let honesty do the heavy lifting.

The story of Day 13 is this: your authentic voice is your most powerful tool. Use it, practice it, and trust that it will carry you further than jargon ever could.

Activity: Think of one lesson you've learned recently. Write it as a short story you could share with a friend instead of a formal explanation.

Reflection: How does shifting to story instead of jargon change the way your message feels?

Day 14: Narrative (Personal Story & Messaging)

On Day 14, we talk about coherence. A mentor once told me, "If your story doesn't make sense to you, it won't make sense to anyone else." At the time, my résumé looked like a patchwork quilt of unrelated roles. Each job seemed disconnected. I feared people would see me as scattered, unfocused, or inconsistent.

But when I stepped back, I noticed a thread running through every role: I was always the one simplifying complexity. Whether I was working in finance, operations, or technology, I kept finding ways to bring order to chaos. That was the story hidden underneath the surface.

Your narrative doesn't have to be linear, but it should be coherent. People don't remember every detail of your journey, but they do remember the theme. Coherence is what makes your story stick, even when the details fade.

I once worked with a client who thought her career zig-zags were a weakness. But when she reframed them as proof of adaptability, resilience, and curiosity, people stopped questioning her path and started admiring it. Coherence doesn't come from sameness—it comes from meaning.

That's the beauty of coherence: it doesn't erase your past, it redeems it. What once felt random becomes part of a purposeful arc. Every role, every pivot, even every failure can serve the larger story when you discover the thread that connects them.

Coherence also builds trust. When people can follow the throughline in your story, they feel grounded in who you are and what you stand for. They know what to expect from you, even if your career takes unexpected turns. Consistency of theme is more powerful than consistency of title.

And coherence frees you from comparison. You don't have to measure your story against anyone else's path, because you're not walking theirs. Your thread is uniquely yours, and once you can name it, you stop apologizing for your journey and start owning it with clarity.

Day 14 is about connecting the dots. The question isn't, "Did I follow the perfect path?" but rather, "What thread ties my experiences together?" That thread is your narrative. That's what makes your story resonate.

The story of Day 14 is this: coherence turns randomness into resonance. When you connect the dots, people don't see a mess— they see a message.

Activity: Sketch your career or life journey as a series of dots. Then draw lines connecting them. What patterns emerge?

Reflection: What single thread ties your story together? How can you share it simply?

Day 15: Narrative (Personal Story & Messaging)

Day 15 is about sharing. A client once told me she wanted to wait until her story was 'perfect' before sharing it publicly. She believed people only wanted polished, flawless versions. But in her waiting, the story stayed locked inside her-and the people who needed it most never got to hear it.

When she finally took the leap, something surprising happened. The parts she thought were too messy or embarrassing turned out to be the parts people related to the most. Her vulnerability became her strength, and her courage inspired others more than a perfect story ever could.

We often assume people want polish, but what they really want is honesty. They don't need you to be flawless-they need you to be real. That's what creates trust. That's what turns a story into a bridge instead of a performance.

Think about the people who've influenced you most. Chances are, it wasn't their polished victories that changed you. It was their struggles, their doubts, and their persistence that reminded you you're not alone. Your story can do the same for someone else.

Day 15 is about action. Waiting for perfection silences your voice. Sharing, even imperfectly, multiplies it. The sooner you tell your story, the sooner it begins to live outside of you and do its work in the world.

The story of Day 15 is this: your story is a gift. Don't hide it. Offer it. You'll be surprised by who is waiting to receive it.

Activity: Share one small piece of your story with someone you trust today. Notice how they respond.

Reflection: What shifts in you when your story is spoken out loud instead of kept inside?

What is one piece of your story that you've been holding back out of fear it's not "perfect"?

Who in your circle might need to hear it right now?

How does it feel different when you imagine offering your story as a gift rather than a performance?

[Write here]

_____

_____

_____

_____

Day 16: Path (Direction & Opportunities)

Day 16 is about choices. I remember standing at a crossroads in my career, torn between staying in a safe role or stepping into something uncertain but exciting. The safe role promised stability. The new role promised growth. My heart leaned one way while my fear pulled the other.

That moment taught me something profound: clarity often reveals itself in the tension between fear and desire. Fear tells us to stay comfortable. Desire whispers that we are capable of more. The real question isn't, 'Which is easier?' but 'Which path moves me closer to who I want to become?'

When you're faced with a choice, it's tempting to look for guarantees. But guarantees don't exist. What you can look for is alignment-does this path align with your values, your genius, and your vision? If it does, then uncertainty isn't a sign to stop-it's a sign you're on the right track.

I've seen people stay stuck for years because they kept waiting for absolute certainty. But clarity rarely comes in advance. It grows as you move forward. You find your path by walking it, not by waiting for the fog to lift.

Day 16 is about courage in decision-making. The path doesn't appear all at once-it reveals itself step by step. Your role is to take the first step in the direction of alignment, even if the whole road isn't visible yet.

The story of Day 16 is this: clarity lives in motion. Choosing to move, even imperfectly, is how you discover the path meant for you.

Activity: Think about one decision you've been delaying. Write down the path that aligns most with your values, even if it feels uncertain.

Reflection: What step can you take this week to move toward that path, even without full certainty?

Day 17: Path (Direction & Opportunities)

On Day 17, we focus on missed opportunities. A client once told me with regret about a job she didn't apply for because she felt unqualified. Later, she learned the person who got it had less experience than she did. Her story wasn't about lack of ability—it was about a missed chance caused by self-doubt.

Opportunities don't knock politely. They whisper. They appear disguised as risks or challenges. And often, they slip away if we don't respond. The key is not to chase every opportunity, but to recognize the ones that align with our genius and have the courage to pursue them.

I've missed opportunities myself by hesitating too long, waiting for perfect timing. But life rarely gives us perfect timing. It gives us openings, and clarity grows when we step into them, even if imperfectly.

The truth is, opportunities rarely look obvious in the moment. They often look inconvenient, scary, or messy. But when you look back, those are the moments that shaped your story most. The risk you took. The door you walked through even when you weren't sure what was inside.

I've come to believe that clarity isn't found by sitting still until everything lines up—it's built in motion. When you say yes to an aligned opportunity, even while trembling, you gather information and experience that standing still could never provide. Momentum breeds clarity in ways hesitation never will.

Another client once shared that she almost turned down a speaking engagement because she felt unprepared. At the last moment, she chose to say yes. That single event connected her with new mentors, sparked fresh ideas, and ultimately opened doors to a new career path. None of it would have happened if she had waited to feel "ready." Sometimes the smallest yes reshapes your entire trajectory.

Fear tells us missed opportunities define us. But the truth is, clarity grows when we learn from those misses. Every door we don't walk through teaches us to recognize the next one more clearly. Regret, if used wisely, sharpens our vision. Instead of becoming stuck in the past, we can use those lessons as guideposts for the future.

And here's the paradox: opportunities often look like interruptions. They show up in the middle of our busy plans, disguised as distractions. But when you pause long enough to ask, "Is this aligned with who I'm becoming?" you gain the wisdom to see which interruptions are really invitations.

Day 17 is about reframing opportunities. Instead of asking, "Am I ready for this?" ask, "Is this aligned with who I'm becoming?" That question shifts you from fear to clarity.

The story of Day 17 is this: clarity doesn't come from avoiding missed chances—it comes from recognizing and seizing the next one.

Activity: Write about one opportunity you regret missing. Then write what you would do differently if a similar opportunity appeared tomorrow.

Reflection: How can you train yourself to notice and act on opportunities that align with your genius?

Day 18: Path (Direction & Opportunities)

Day 18 is about crossroads. I once mentored a young professional who was torn between two offers: one was high-paying but uninspiring, the other was aligned with her passions but riskier. She was frozen by the weight of choosing.

We often believe there's one "right" path and fear choosing the wrong one. But clarity grows when you see that both paths shape you in different ways. The decision is not about right versus wrong—it's about alignment versus misalignment.

I asked her, "Which choice helps you grow into the person you want to become?" That question shifted everything. Suddenly, it wasn't about salary or prestige—it was about identity and future self. She chose the risky path, and though it wasn't easy, it grew her in ways money never could.

Crossroads test our clarity. They force us to ask, "What story do I want to tell about this season of my life?" That question often reveals more truth than a pros-and-cons list ever could.

I've learned that indecision itself carries a cost. When you linger too long at the crossroads, you burn energy without moving forward. Even a difficult path walked with clarity is more life-giving than standing still in fear. Choosing doesn't guarantee ease, but it guarantees momentum.

And here's the paradox: the more you face crossroads, the more resilient you become. Each decision builds your capacity to trust yourself, to rely on your values, and to see clarity in uncertainty. Over time, you stop dreading crossroads and start welcoming them as opportunities to practice the kind of leader—and person—you're becoming.

Day 18 is about embracing crossroads not as threats but as invitations. They invite you to clarify your values, your genius, and your direction.

The story of Day 18 is this: crossroads are not signs of confusion—they are opportunities for clarity. Your choice writes the next chapter of your story.

Activity: Think about a current or past crossroads in your life. What story would you be proud to tell about the choice you made?

Reflection: How does this perspective shift the way you see difficult decisions?

Day 19: Path (Direction & Opportunities)

Day 19 is about detours. A friend once dreamed of becoming a teacher but ended up in corporate sales. At first, she thought she had failed her path. But years later, she realized the detour had sharpened her skills in communication, persuasion, and leadership—skills she now uses as an educator.

Detours feel frustrating because they don't fit the plan we imagined. But clarity often hides in detours. They give us experiences, lessons, and strengths we wouldn't have gained otherwise.

I once found myself in a job I never planned on taking, convinced it was a waste of time. Looking back, it taught me resilience, resourcefulness, and how to lead people under pressure. The detour wasn't a waste—it was preparation.

We treat detours as failures, but they are often the chapters that give our story depth. Without them, our path might be smoother, but it would also be shallower.

The truth is, detours expose us to perspectives we'd never seek on our own. They stretch us into unfamiliar roles, introduce us to people we wouldn't have met, and give us a vantage point we can carry into the future. Sometimes the very insights that set us apart as leaders come from the roads we didn't mean to travel.

Detours also humble us. They remind us we are not fully in control of timing or outcomes. That humility builds empathy. Leaders who have walked through detours tend to listen better, guide with more patience, and see the value in unconventional journeys. What feels like delay can actually deepen our humanity.

I've seen entire careers redefined by reframing detours. One client was laid off twice in five years and thought it disqualified her from leadership. But when she reframed those seasons as proof of adaptability and reinvention, recruiters suddenly saw her as someone who could lead in uncertain times. Her detours became her credibility.

Another gift of detours is hidden creativity. When your original path is blocked, you're forced to invent new ways forward. Those innovations often outlast the detour itself. What you build in the margins sometimes becomes the main road.

And perhaps most importantly, detours prepare us for future opportunities we can't yet see. Skills you thought were irrelevant suddenly become your advantage in a new role or season. What once felt like a diversion reveals itself as a foundation.

Day 19 is about shifting how we see detours. Instead of asking, "Why did this happen to me?" ask, "What did this path give me that I wouldn't have otherwise?" That question changes everything.

The story of Day 19 is this: detours don't take you off the path—they build the path. Clarity comes when you honor them as part of your journey.

Activity: Write about one detour in your life. What unexpected skills or strengths did it give you?

Reflection: How does seeing your detour as preparation shift the way you view your story?

Day 20: Path (Direction & Opportunities)

On Day 20, we talk about momentum. Clarity is not a lightning bolt—it's a slow burn that builds as you keep moving forward. I once worked on a long project that felt overwhelming in the beginning. But as I took small, consistent steps, momentum built and clarity grew.

Momentum works like compound interest. Each small step seems insignificant, but over time, the accumulation creates something powerful. You don't need giant leaps to build clarity—you need steady movement.

I've seen people paralyze themselves by waiting for perfect clarity before starting. But clarity doesn't come before action—it comes because of action. Each step illuminates the next.

The beauty of momentum is that it doesn't just create progress—it creates confidence. The more steps you take, the more capable you feel. That confidence becomes fuel for the journey ahead.

Momentum also has a contagious quality. When you consistently take action, others notice and begin to move with you. Teams, communities, and even families are often waiting for someone to set the pace. One person's steady rhythm can spark collective movement.

What's overlooked is how momentum survives setbacks. When you've built steady forward motion, a single obstacle doesn't stop you—it just slows you temporarily. Momentum gives you resilience, because it's easier to restart when you've already built a habit of progress.

I've worked with clients who spent years "planning to start" but gained more traction in two months of imperfect action than in two years of preparation. They discovered that clarity is rarely found in the planning stage—it's revealed in the doing. Momentum is the bridge between intention and insight.

And here's the paradox: the hardest part of momentum is the beginning. Starting feels heavy, but once you've taken a few steps, energy builds and carries you forward. That's why the first move— no matter how small—is often the most important.

Day 20 is about trusting the process. You don't need to see the whole road to know you're moving in the right direction. Every small step matters more than you think.

The story of Day 20 is this: clarity grows with momentum. The more you move, the clearer the path becomes.

Activity: Choose one small step you can take today toward a goal. Don't wait for perfect clarity—let the step itself create it.

Reflection: How does focusing on momentum instead of certainty change the way you see your path?

What is one area of your life where you've been waiting for clarity before acting?

How might one small step today create the momentum you need?

What past experience reminds you that clarity grew after you started moving, not before?

How would your confidence grow if you trusted progress over perfection this week?

[Write here]

_____

_____

_____

_____

Day 21: Community (Relationships & Amplifiers)

Day 21 is about the people who see us more clearly than we see ourselves. I once had a mentor who consistently told me, 'You have a gift for clarity.' At the time, I shrugged it off. I thought he was just being kind. But over the years, I realized he was pointing out something I had overlooked in myself.

We often dismiss what others see in us because it feels too ordinary. But ordinary to you can be extraordinary to others. Sometimes community is the mirror that reflects your genius back to you when you've forgotten to look.

I've coached people who discovered their greatest strengths only after someone else named them. A colleague saying, 'You're the one who keeps us calm,' or a friend noting, 'You always connect people,' can become a revelation if you're willing to hear it.

The danger is that we often ignore these reflections, dismissing them as flattery. But the truth is, they are often accurate. Others can see us from angles we cannot. Their perspective can become a compass if we take it seriously.

Day 21 is about listening. Not just to your own voice, but to the voices of those who care about you. Their words can uncover clarity you didn't know was hiding in plain sight.

The story of Day 21 is this: your community is not just your audience-it's your mirror. Sometimes the clearest view of your genius comes through the eyes of others.

Activity: Ask three people close to you to describe what they see as your greatest strength. Write down their answers without dismissing them.

Reflection: What common themes appear in their responses? How do they align with the genius you've been uncovering?

Day 22: Community (Relationships & Amplifiers)

On Day 22, we focus on mentors. I once worked under a leader who didn't just manage projects-he cultivated people. He taught me that mentorship isn't about giving answers but about asking better questions. His guidance shaped me in ways I still carry today.

Mentors expand our clarity because they offer perspective rooted in experience. They've walked paths we haven't, faced challenges we're only beginning to see, and can point out pitfalls we might miss. Their role is not to hand us a map but to hand us a compass.

I've found that the best mentors don't make you dependent on them. Instead, they empower you to trust your own judgment. They remind you that clarity isn't borrowed-it's built.

The challenge is that many people wait passively for mentors to appear. But mentorship is often something you cultivate. It begins with curiosity, humility, and the courage to ask someone you admire to share their perspective.

Day 22 is about seeking and valuing mentorship. You don't need to wait for the perfect guide to arrive. Look around-who already inspires you, and how can you invite their perspective into your journey?

The story of Day 22 is this: mentorship is less about hierarchy and more about relationship. Seek it, nurture it, and let it sharpen your clarity.

Activity: Identify one person you admire and ask them a simple question about their journey. Begin building that connection today.

Reflection: What did their perspective reveal to you about your own path?

Day 23: Community (Relationships & Amplifiers)

Day 23 is about allies. These are the people who walk alongside you, not above you. I remember a season when I was building something new and felt completely overwhelmed. It wasn't a mentor who carried me through-it was peers. Friends who checked in, who encouraged me, who reminded me I wasn't alone.

Allies amplify clarity because they remind you of your capacity when you forget it. They are the ones who say, 'You've got this,' when your own voice is filled with doubt. Their belief becomes fuel.

Unlike mentors, allies don't have more experience than you-they're simply in the trenches with you. They share the journey, the challenges, and the small victories. Their power comes from empathy and solidarity.

I've seen communities thrive not because of one great leader but because of allies who supported one another. The collective belief created momentum none of them could have built alone.

Day 23 is about valuing the allies in your life. They may not have the answers, but they give you strength to keep walking the path. And often, their support is what keeps clarity alive in seasons of doubt.

The story of Day 23 is this: clarity is not a solo pursuit. It is sustained by the allies who remind you that you don't have to walk alone.

Activity: Reach out to one ally today and thank them for the role they play in your journey. Be specific about the clarity they've helped you keep.

Reflection: How does acknowledging your allies shift your sense of community and strength?

Day 24: Community (Relationships & Amplifiers)

Day 24 is about amplifiers. These are the people who don't just support you privately but champion you publicly. I once worked with a colleague who consistently mentioned my name in rooms I wasn't in. Her advocacy opened doors I could never have opened alone.

Amplifiers are powerful because they expand your reach. They take your clarity and multiply it by sharing it with others. They aren't just cheerleaders-they are connectors who put your genius in front of the right eyes.

The mistake many people make is waiting for amplifiers to appear. But amplifiers often emerge when you've been consistent in showing up with clarity. People are more likely to amplify what they trust, and trust is built over time.

I've seen lives and careers transformed because of one amplifier who believed in someone's story and was willing to share it widely. Their influence became a catalyst for opportunities that might have taken years otherwise.

Day 24 is about recognizing and cultivating amplifiers. They are a gift, but they are also drawn to consistency and courage. When you share your story boldly, you make it easier for amplifiers to carry it further.

The story of Day 24 is this: amplifiers don't create your genius-they project it. Your clarity becomes their message, and together you reach further than you could alone.

Activity: Identify one amplifier in your life-someone who has spoken up for you or shared your work. Thank them for their role in your journey.

Reflection: What could you do to make it easier for amplifiers to share your story?

Day 25: Community (Relationships & Amplifiers)

On Day 25, we integrate the lessons of community. Over the past days, you've explored mirrors, mentors, allies, and amplifiers. Each plays a unique role in shaping your clarity, but together they create something even stronger: a network of belief.

I once worked with a team where every individual was talented, but what made them powerful wasn't their skills—it was their belief in each other. That belief created an atmosphere where ideas thrived, risks felt safe, and clarity multiplied.

Community is not just about support—it's about multiplication. Alone, you can carry clarity for a while. But with community, clarity becomes exponential. Others see angles you miss, strengthen you when you're weak, and push you when you hesitate.

The mistake many of us make is trying to build clarity in isolation. We think genius is a solo act. But clarity thrives in connection. The more you invest in relationships, the more sustainable your clarity becomes.

And here's the deeper truth: community doesn't just shape what you create—it shapes who you become. When you're surrounded by people who believe in you, you start believing in yourself at a higher level. Their vision of your potential often stretches farther than your own, pulling you into growth you wouldn't reach alone.

At its best, community becomes a mirror and a multiplier. It reflects back your strengths while magnifying your impact. The more you pour into it, the more it pours back into you, creating a cycle of clarity that outlasts any single moment or achievement.

Day 25 is about celebrating the people who shape you. Your genius doesn't exist in a vacuum—it exists in a web of relationships that amplify it. Recognizing that web is both humbling and empowering.

The story of Day 25 is this: clarity is communal. It grows strongest when it is shared, supported, and multiplied through others.

Activity: Write down the names of three people who have shaped your clarity. Reach out to one today and express your gratitude.

Reflection: How does acknowledging the role of community deepen your sense of clarity and responsibility?

Day 26: Focus (Simplifying & Prioritizing)

Day 26 is about the power of saying no. For years, I said yes to every request, believing it was the key to success. More projects, more visibility, more approval. But what it really gave me was exhaustion. My clarity was buried under commitments that didn't truly matter to me.

The turning point came when I realized every yes is also a no. Saying yes to one thing means saying no to something else—often to the things that matter most. Once I understood this, I began to treat yes as sacred. A yes should only go to what aligns with your genius and your path.

I once watched a leader decline an opportunity that would have made her more visible but would have pulled her away from her core mission. People thought she was crazy to turn it down. But months later, her clarity had created an opportunity even better aligned with her vision. Her no had made space for the right yes.

Focus is not about doing everything—it's about doing the right things. It's about curating your commitments, so your time and energy go where they matter most. Without no, clarity gets diluted until it disappears.

Day 26 is about reclaiming your no. It's about remembering that clarity isn't just about what you pursue—it's about what you protect yourself from. Your no is not a weakness. It is strength in disguise.

The truth is, every no has a cost in the moment—discomfort, misunderstanding, even disapproval. But the cost of endless yeses is far greater: burnout, regret, and the slow erosion of your genius. Choosing short-term discomfort often protects you from long-term drift.

No is also a teacher. Each time you use it, you learn more about your values, your boundaries, and your true direction. Over time, you develop a sharper filter. You stop chasing opportunities just because they're available and start choosing them because they're aligned.

I've seen teams thrive when they collectively practice no. Instead of piling on projects to look busy, they chose a handful of priorities and declined everything else. The result wasn't less productivity—it was better productivity, fueled by clarity and focus.

And here's the paradox: no actually makes you more generous. When you stop scattering your energy across everything, you can give your best self to the commitments you do accept. People don't just get more of you—they get the best of you.

One leader I coached began practicing no by turning down just one request a week. At first, it felt awkward. But soon, she noticed her calendar opening up, her creativity returning, and her stress shrinking. Her no became a doorway back to herself.

Saying no also builds trust. People may not always like it, but they come to respect it. They know that when you say yes, you mean it— that your word is anchored, not scattered. That kind of integrity deepens your influence far more than constant availability ever could.

The story of Day 26 is this: every no creates room for a better yes. Protect your clarity by choosing carefully what you allow in.

Activity: Identify one commitment that doesn't align with your genius. Practice saying no, even if it feels uncomfortable.

Reflection: What clarity did you feel after protecting your time with a no?

Day 27: Focus (Simplifying & Prioritizing)

Day 27 is about pruning. Think of your life as a tree. Growth isn't just about adding more branches—it's also about cutting back the ones that no longer serve the tree's strength. Without pruning, even the healthiest tree becomes tangled and weak.

I once met a professional who was proud of his long list of responsibilities. But when we looked closer, half of them drained him. They were branches sucking away his energy. Once he pruned them, he had space to grow stronger in the areas that mattered most.

Pruning doesn't always look dramatic. Sometimes it's as simple as letting go of a task you've outgrown, a relationship that no longer aligns, or a goal that no longer fits your path. The act of release is what creates space for clarity to flourish.

We often hold on to too much out of fear—fear of disappointing others, fear of missing out, fear of being seen as incapable. But pruning is not loss. It's intentional focus. It's the decision to choose depth over breadth.

I've learned that pruning also requires honesty. It means facing the uncomfortable truth that not everything you're doing is fruitful. Some projects once served a purpose but no longer do. Some relationships once gave life but now drain it. Pruning is an act of self-leadership where you admit, "This season has ended," and free yourself to step into what's next.

Pruning also teaches humility. Trees don't prune themselves to impress anyone—they prune to survive and thrive. In the same way, pruning isn't about looking productive or polished; it's about building strength where it matters most. Leaders who prune show their teams that it's okay to stop doing things that no longer serve the mission. That kind of modeling frees others to do the same.

And pruning is cyclical. Just as a tree needs regular pruning to remain healthy, so do we. One season of pruning doesn't last forever. Life will always add new branches, new commitments, and new opportunities. Regularly asking, "What needs to be released right now?" keeps your clarity alive and your growth sustainable.

I've also seen pruning create unexpected joy. At first, letting go feels like loss. But soon, the relief arrives—the extra space in your schedule, the lighter emotional load, the renewed sense of energy. That joy isn't accidental. It's the fruit of living aligned with clarity rather than entangled in noise.

Ultimately, pruning is an act of courage. It takes boldness to step away from something familiar, even if it no longer serves you. But every time you choose to prune, you make space for something better to grow. And that better growth is where clarity always leads.

Day 27 is about courage in letting go. Clarity isn't found by adding more branches—it's revealed when you clear away what's in the way.

The story of Day 27 is this: pruning is not about less—it's about better. Focus grows when you release what no longer serves you.

Activity: List three things you're doing right now that no longer serve your clarity. Choose one to prune today.

Reflection: How does pruning change the way you feel about your time, energy, and direction?

Day 28: Focus (Simplifying & Prioritizing)

Day 28 is about distraction. We live in a world where distraction is the norm. Notifications, endless scrolling, constant noise. I used to believe I could multitask my way to clarity, but all I really created was shallow focus and mediocre results.

The truth is, multitasking isn't mastery-it's fragmentation. Every time you split your attention, you dilute your genius. Deep clarity requires deep focus, and deep focus requires shutting out the noise.

I once worked with a team that instituted 'focus hours.' No emails, no meetings, just uninterrupted work. Productivity and creativity skyrocketed. What changed wasn't their talent-it was their focus.

Distraction is clarity's thief. It steals not just your time but your best energy. The cost of distraction is higher than we admit, and the reward of focus is greater than we imagine.

Day 28 is about reclaiming focus in a distracted world. Clarity doesn't compete with noise-it requires you to turn the noise down so your genius can be heard.

The story of Day 28 is this: focus is the discipline of choosing what matters most and giving it your full attention. Everything else can wait.

Activity: Choose one block of two hours today where you eliminate distractions-no phone, no email, no interruptions. Notice what changes.

Reflection: What did you accomplish in your distraction-free time that surprised you?

Day 29: Focus (Simplifying & Prioritizing)

Day 29 is about priorities. Early in my career, I treated every task as equally urgent. My to-do list was a monster that grew faster than I could keep up with. The result? Burnout and frustration. Then a mentor taught me the simple art of ranking my priorities.

He said, 'Not everything is equally important. If you treat it all as urgent, you'll spend your life on what doesn't matter.' That advice changed how I approached my days. Instead of drowning in tasks, I began to ask: what are the few things that truly move me forward?

I discovered that clarity comes when you separate the essential from the noise. The urgent often screams the loudest, but it's rarely the most important. The important is quieter, but it's what builds lasting progress.

I've seen leaders transform their lives simply by focusing on their top three priorities each day. They didn't work longer hours. They worked clearer hours. And clarity, not time, became their greatest asset.

Day 29 is about simplifying priorities. It's not about doing more, it's about doing what matters most. When you align your actions with your priorities, your clarity sharpens like a lens coming into focus.

The story of Day 29 is this: clarity is not built by doing everything- it's built by doing the right things in the right order.

Activity: Write down your top three priorities for today. Focus only on those and let the rest wait.

Reflection: How does narrowing your focus to the essential change your productivity and peace of mind?

Day 30: Focus (Simplifying & Prioritizing)

On Day 30, we celebrate integration. Over the past 30 days, you've uncovered your genius, aligned your environment, reshaped your narrative, clarified your path, built community, and practiced focus. Each piece on its own is powerful, but together they form something greater—clarity as a way of life.

I've watched people go through this journey and emerge not as someone different, but as someone more themselves. Clarity doesn't make you someone new—it makes you more of who you already are, with less noise and more intention.

The journey isn't about perfection. There will still be days of fog, doubt, and distraction. But now you have tools, stories, and practices that can bring you back to center when the noise threatens to take over.

One of the greatest shifts I've seen in people is confidence. Not the loud, boastful kind, but the quiet confidence of knowing who you are, what matters most, and how to stay true to it. That's the gift clarity gives.

Integration also brings peace. When your actions, words, and values line up, you no longer live in conflict with yourself. The energy once wasted on trying to be everything for everyone gets reclaimed. You begin to feel lighter, freer, and more at ease in your own skin. That peace radiates outward, shaping the way others experience you.

Another fruit of integration is influence. Clarity isn't just for you— it spills over. Teams work differently when a leader models clarity. Families breathe differently when parents create environments of calm and focus. Communities thrive when individuals bring their genius with alignment. Your personal clarity becomes a gift to others.

Day 30 also reminds us that integration is never "finished." Just as a garden must be tended season after season, clarity must be revisited. New roles, challenges, and opportunities will arise, and each one will test the clarity you've built. But now, instead of starting from scratch, you return to practices that ground you. Integration is both the harvest and the planting for what comes next.

Finally, integration unlocks joy. Gratitude and clarity walk hand in hand. When you take time to celebrate progress instead of obsessing over what's left undone, you create room for joy. That joy fuels momentum. It reminds you that clarity isn't just useful—it's beautiful.

Integration also gives you perspective. Looking back, you'll realize the power wasn't just in the big breakthroughs, but in the accumulation of small, faithful steps. Each practice, each reflection, each moment of courage built a foundation stronger than you imagined.

And integration invites legacy. The clarity you've built doesn't end with you—it shapes how you lead, how you love, and what you leave behind. Your 30-day journey is just the beginning of a ripple effect that will touch people you may never meet, long after the 30 days are over.

Day 30 is about gratitude. Gratitude for the progress you've made, the insights you've gathered, and the clarity you've built. Gratitude multiplies clarity because it shifts your focus from what's missing to what's possible.

The story of Day 30 is this: clarity is not a destination—it's a practice. You've begun the journey, and every day forward is another chance to live with more focus, more purpose, and more lightness.

Activity: Write a short letter to yourself, celebrating the clarity you've built over the past 30 days. Keep it as a reminder for future seasons.

Reflection: How does gratitude for your journey shift the way you see your next steps?

Looking back on the past 30 days, what are you most proud of?

Where did you experience the biggest shift in your clarity?

How will you carry these practices into the next season of your life?

Who else might benefit from the clarity you've built, and how will you share it?

[Write here]

_____

_____

_____

_____

Part II – Deepening the Practice

Next, you'll learn how to apply clarity in more complex situations. Through expanded lessons and case studies, you'll discover how clarity transforms not just your personal habits, but also how teams and organizations operate.

Day 31: Content Engine (Consistency & Creation)

Day 31 begins a new phase: turning clarity into content. In Part I, you uncovered your genius. Now it's time to share it. Content is not about flooding the world with noise—it's about offering meaningful signals that others can trust. The first step is showing up consistently.

I once worked with a client who resisted posting online because she feared she had nothing new to say. But when she began writing weekly reflections, her voice grew stronger. The practice of showing up built both her confidence and her audience.

Consistency is more important than brilliance. People don't need perfect essays every day—they need reminders that you are present, trustworthy, and committed to sharing value.

Think of your content as conversation starters, not final answers. You don't have to have the whole map figured out to invite someone into your journey. You just have to show up with something honest and useful.

The more you create, the more patterns you'll see. You'll notice what resonates, what sparks dialogue, and what begins to define your voice. But none of this happens if you don't start showing up consistently.

Consistency also creates trust over time. An audience that sees you show up week after week learns to rely on your presence. Even if they don't read every post, the steady rhythm builds familiarity. Familiarity is the soil where trust grows.

The act of creating regularly also sharpens your own thinking. Writing, speaking, or recording forces you to process your clarity in ways that private reflection cannot. As you put your thoughts into words, vague ideas become sharp insights, and those insights become part of your signature voice.

And here's the hidden gift: content doesn't just reach others—it reshapes you. Each post, article, or video is a marker of growth, a record of your evolving clarity. Looking back months later, you'll see how far you've come simply because you kept showing up.

The story of Day 31 is this: consistency builds clarity in public. By creating regularly, you transform your private genius into shared value.

Activity: Choose one platform where you'll share your voice. Commit to posting once a week, no matter how small the contribution.

Reflection: How does consistency shift your confidence in sharing your clarity with others?

Day 32: Content Engine (Consistency & Creation)

Day 32 is about simplicity. Early in my journey, I thought content had to be long, polished, and elaborate. I spent hours crafting posts that few people read. What I learned is that simple, clear messages often travel further than complicated ones.

People don't remember paragraphs—they remember sentences. A clear sentence like 'Clarity beats complexity' will stick with someone long after a detailed explanation fades.

Think of the content that impacted you most. Chances are, it wasn't long or fancy—it was clear, relatable, and easy to apply. That's the power of simplicity.

Simplicity doesn't mean dumbing down your message. It means stripping away what isn't essential so the core truth shines through.

When your content is simple, people share it. They quote it. They make it part of their own story. That's when your genius multiplies beyond you.

The story of Day 32 is this: clarity thrives on simplicity. The simpler your message, the further it can go.

Activity: Take one idea you've been overexplaining. Rewrite it as a single clear sentence you could share with a friend.

Reflection: How does reducing complexity sharpen the impact of your message?

Day 33: Content Engine (Consistency & Creation)

Day 33 is about rhythm. Just as in Part I we talked about rituals for clarity, now we create rituals for content. A writer I admire sets aside one hour every morning to write, no matter what. Some days it produces brilliance, other days just a paragraph. But the rhythm is what matters.

Rhythm creates trust—not only with your audience, but with yourself. Each time you show up, you reinforce the identity of being someone who shares value.

Without rhythm, content becomes a chore, something you squeeze in when you can. With rhythm, it becomes a practice that sustains you as much as it sustains others.

Your rhythm doesn't have to look like anyone else's. It might be writing once a week, recording a short video every Friday, or sharing a thought every morning. The point isn't volume—it's consistency shaped by rhythm.

When you create a rhythm, you stop negotiating with yourself about whether to show up. It becomes part of who you are.

The story of Day 33 is this: rhythm builds reliability. And reliability builds trust.

Activity: Choose one rhythm for your content creation—time, place, and frequency. Put it in your calendar and honor it as you would a meeting.

Reflection: How does rhythm make it easier to sustain your clarity in public?

Day 34: Content Engine (Consistency & Creation)

Day 34 is about resonance. Not all content resonates equally, and that's okay. I once wrote an article I thought was brilliant, and it landed with silence. Weeks later, I shared a simple reflection I almost didn't post, and it sparked dozens of conversations.

Resonance isn't about what impresses you—it's about what connects with others. Sometimes the smallest stories carry the greatest impact because they touch something universal.

To create resonance, you need to pay attention. Notice which posts, stories, or reflections draw responses. Look for the moments where people say, 'That's exactly what I needed to hear.'

Resonance grows when you let go of trying to be impressive and instead aim to be honest. Honesty connects. Perfection distances.

The more you notice resonance, the better you'll become at shaping your content around what matters most to your audience.

The story of Day 34 is this: resonance is about connection, not performance. Connection is what builds community around your clarity.

Activity: Review your last few pieces of shared content. Which ones sparked conversation? Which ones fell flat? Write down what you notice.

Reflection: How can you create more of what resonates instead of chasing what looks impressive?

Day 35: Content Engine (Consistency & Creation)

Day 35 is about courage. Sharing your voice in public can feel vulnerable. You may fear judgment, criticism, or being misunderstood. But clarity grows stronger when tested in public spaces.

I once hesitated to share a story about failure, worried it would make me look weak. Instead, it became one of the most appreciated things I ever shared. People connected because it was real, not polished.

Courage doesn't mean the fear disappears. It means you choose to show up anyway, trusting that your authenticity will matter more than your perfection.

Every creator, leader, or thought-sharer faces fear. What separates those who grow is not the absence of fear but the willingness to act despite it.

When you lead with courage, you give others permission to do the same. Your voice becomes not only content but encouragement for someone else to step forward.

The story of Day 35 is this: courage is contagious. The more you share with honesty, the braver others will become in their own clarity.

Activity: Share one piece of content that feels slightly uncomfortable but true. Notice the response it creates.

Reflection: How does sharing with courage shift your sense of connection to your audience?

Day 36: Content Engine (Depth & Development)

Day 36 is about depth. When you first start creating, your content may skim the surface. That's natural. But clarity deepens when you dig beneath the obvious. Depth comes from sharing not only what you know but how you've lived it.

I once followed a writer who transformed my perspective. At first, his posts were clever, but shallow. Then one day he shared the story of his first business failure and what it taught him. That post changed everything. His honesty and depth pulled me in far more than his polished advice ever had.

Depth doesn't mean being long-winded—it means being willing to go beyond the cliché. Instead of 'failure builds character,' share the exact moment failure shook you, the lessons you took, and how you grew. Specificity creates resonance.

Many creators fear going deep because they think it makes them vulnerable. And it does. But that vulnerability is often what makes your content trustworthy. People don't need perfect—they need real.

As you grow in content creation, look for ways to add layers to your stories. Peel back the first explanation and ask, 'What's beneath this?' That's where the depth lives.

The story of Day 36 is this: depth creates distinction. When you go deeper, you stop sounding like everyone else and start sounding like yourself.

Activity: Take one story you've shared before and rewrite it with more detail. Add the emotions, the lessons, and the turning point you left out before.

Reflection: How does sharing with depth change the way people connect with your message?

Day 37: Content Engine (Depth & Development)

Day 37 is about themes. As you create consistently, you'll start noticing patterns in your content. These themes are the backbone of your voice. They give your audience a sense of what to expect and help you stay anchored in your clarity.

When I first started writing, I felt pressure to cover every topic under the sun. But the more I focused, the stronger my voice became. I realized I was circling the same themes: clarity, simplicity, and leadership. Those themes became my signature.

Themes are like threads woven through your content. They connect individual pieces into a tapestry that tells a bigger story.

You don't need dozens of themes. In fact, too many can dilute your clarity. Three to five is often enough. Think of them as pillars that hold up your voice.

When you identify your themes, you create both freedom and focus. Freedom, because you don't have to reinvent yourself every time. Focus, because you know what matters most to you and your audience.

I've also noticed that themes build trust over time. When your audience repeatedly encounters the same core ideas, they begin to associate you with those values. Your themes become a promise—that when they return to your work, they'll find guidance in the areas that matter most to them.

And here's the beauty: themes also evolve as you do. The pillars you start with may grow deeper or shift slightly as your experience widens. What matters is not that your themes stay frozen, but that they remain authentic reflections of your genius and the clarity you're practicing in real time.

The story of Day 37 is this: themes give your content coherence. They transform scattered posts into a body of work that builds trust over time.

Activity: Review your recent content. Highlight three recurring themes you naturally come back to. Write them down as your pillars.

Reflection: How do these themes reflect your genius and give direction to your content??

Day 38: Content Engine (Depth & Development)

Day 38 is about repurposing. One of the biggest mistakes creators make is thinking they need to reinvent the wheel every time. But clarity is reinforced through repetition. Repurposing allows you to reach more people without burning out.

I once gave a talk at a small workshop. Months later, I turned the same material into a blog post, then into a short video, then into a podcast episode. Each time, the audience grew. The core idea didn't change, but the format did.

Repurposing is not laziness—it's strategy. People need to hear your message multiple times, in multiple ways, before it sticks. By repurposing, you honor both your time and your audience's learning.

The beauty of repurposing is that it makes your content more inclusive. Some people love reading. Others prefer listening. Others need visuals. Repurposing lets you serve them all.

Day 38 reminds us that clarity is not about constant invention but about consistent reinforcement. Repurposing multiplies your impact without multiplying your workload.

The story of Day 38 is this: repetition builds reputation. The more ways you share your message, the more it becomes anchored in people's minds.

Activity: Take one idea you've already shared and reframe it in a new format—turn a post into a video, or a talk into a blog.

Reflection: What did you notice about how the same idea reached people differently in a new form?

Day 39: Content Engine (Depth & Development)

Day 39 is about feedback. As you create, your community will respond. Some feedback will be encouraging, some will be critical. Both are valuable if you know how to use them.

I once shared a story I loved, but a reader commented that it felt confusing. At first, I was defensive. But when I reread it, I saw their point. Their feedback helped me refine my voice.

Feedback is not a verdict—it's data. It tells you how your message is landing, not whether it's worth sharing. Use it to sharpen, not silence, your voice.

The danger is letting feedback define you. Not every comment is valid, and not every opinion deserves equal weight. The key is discerning patterns—when multiple people say the same thing, it's worth paying attention.

Day 39 is about humility. Clarity grows when you're open enough to listen, but grounded enough not to be swayed by every opinion.

The story of Day 39 is this: feedback is a mirror, not a cage. Use it to refine your clarity, not to restrict it.

Activity: Ask three people for feedback on something you've shared recently. Look for patterns rather than isolated opinions.

Reflection: How does treating feedback as data rather than judgment shift the way you receive it?

Day 40: Content Engine (Depth & Development)

Day 40 is about sustainability. It's easy to sprint when you're excited, but clarity is built over the long haul. Content creation is a marathon, not a sprint.

I once knew a creator who posted daily for a month, then burned out and disappeared for six months. His audience didn't need daily brilliance—they needed steady reliability.

Sustainability comes from pacing yourself. It's better to post once a week for a year than every day for a month. Longevity beats intensity when it comes to building trust.

Part of sustainability is protecting your energy. If content creation feels like a burden, step back and ask: how can I make this lighter, simpler, more aligned with my genius?

Day 40 reminds us that clarity is not about one viral moment but about steady contribution. The people who build lasting impact are the ones who keep showing up, long after the excitement fades.

The story of Day 40 is this: sustainability is the secret to influence. Show up at a pace you can maintain, and your clarity will compound over time.

Activity: Set a realistic pace for your content. Decide how often you can sustainably create and commit to it.

Reflection: How does focusing on sustainability change your approach to sharing your clarity?

Reflection Journal

Where in your life or work have you sprinted only to burn out?

What would it look like to trade intensity for longevity in your creative process?

How can you protect your energy while still showing up consistently for your audience or team?

What is one small adjustment you could make this week to create at a pace you can sustain for the long haul?

[Write here]

_____

_____

_____

_____

Day 41: Building Authority (Credibility & Multipliers)

Day 41 is about credibility. In the early stages of sharing content, people may enjoy your insights, but credibility is what makes them trust you. Trust doesn't come from claims—it comes from consistency, results, and alignment between your words and actions.

I remember working with a consultant who shared brilliant posts online but failed to deliver on deadlines with clients. Her content drew people in, but her lack of follow-through eroded credibility. Words alone cannot carry authority.

Credibility is built when your audience sees your message reflected in your actions. When you talk about clarity and they see you living with focus. When you share about courage and they see you taking risks yourself. Alignment builds authority.

The good news is credibility doesn't require perfection. People don't expect flawless leaders—they expect authentic ones. Credibility is strengthened when you own your mistakes and demonstrate how you've learned from them.

I've seen credibility deepen most when leaders embody patience. In a world obsessed with quick wins, the willingness to stay steady, deliver consistently, and keep promises over time makes you stand out. Credibility isn't earned in a single post or presentation—it's built brick by brick, each aligned action stacking on the last.

And credibility doesn't just serve your audience; it serves you. When you live in alignment, you carry less internal tension. You no longer feel pressure to perform or project an image. Your message flows more naturally because it's grounded in reality, and that ease makes your influence even stronger.

Day 41 is about remembering that authority doesn't come from titles or likes. It comes from trust, and trust comes from integrity between your message and your life.

The story of Day 41 is this: credibility is the bridge between content and authority. Without it, your message collapses. With it, your influence expands.

Activity: Identify one area where your actions and words feel misaligned. Take one step today to close that gap.

Reflection: How does alignment between your message and actions strengthen your credibility?

Day 42: Building Authority (Credibility & Multipliers)

Day 42 is about expertise. People often hesitate to claim authority because they don't feel like "the expert." But expertise is not about knowing everything—it's about being a step ahead and willing to share what you know.

I once coached someone who was brilliant in her field but kept downplaying her voice. She said, "I'm not the top expert, so why should people listen to me?" My answer was simple: people don't need the world's number one expert—they need someone who can guide them one step further.

Authority grows when you share from where you are. You don't have to wait until you've mastered everything. Share what you've learned, the mistakes you've made, and the lessons that helped you move forward. That honesty builds more trust than pretending to have it all figured out.

The paradox of expertise is that the more you share, the more you grow. Teaching forces you to clarify your own thinking. As you guide others, you strengthen your own authority.

I've found that expertise is best measured not by titles or credentials but by impact. If your knowledge helps someone solve a problem, move past a fear, or see something more clearly, then you are already operating as an expert in their eyes. Your willingness to share generously becomes the real marker of your authority.

And the truth is, expertise is always evolving. Today's lessons prepare you to guide someone now, while tomorrow's experiences will prepare you to guide others later. Authority is not a static crown you wear—it's a living process of walking a step ahead and inviting others along the way.

Day 42 is about owning your place in the journey. You may not be the top expert, but you are an expert in your experience, and that matters deeply to someone just starting out.

The story of Day 42 is this: expertise is not perfection. Authority grows when you share what you've already walked through with honesty and generosity.

Activity: Write down three lessons you've learned in your field that you could teach someone a step behind you.

Reflection: How does claiming your expertise shift your confidence in your authority?

Day 43: Building Authority (Credibility & Multipliers)

Day 43 is about proof. In a world filled with voices, authority requires evidence. Proof can come in many forms—results, testimonials, case studies, or even your own story of transformation.

I once worked with a coach who struggled to attract clients until she began sharing stories of people she had helped. The moment she offered tangible examples, her authority grew. Proof gives your audience confidence that your message isn't just theory—it works.

The most powerful proof is often the simplest. A before-and-after story. A specific result someone experienced. A measurable change you helped create. These stories build trust faster than any abstract claim.

But proof isn't only external. Sometimes your own journey is the most compelling evidence. Sharing how you moved from confusion to clarity makes your authority relatable, not distant.

Proof also protects against doubt. In a noisy digital world where anyone can claim expertise, evidence distinguishes you from empty promises. When you show receipts—whether it's data, transformation stories, or tangible outcomes—you invite your audience to believe not because you say so, but because they can see so.

I've noticed that proof doesn't have to be grand to be persuasive. Leaders sometimes dismiss small wins, thinking they're not impressive enough to share. But small, specific victories are often more believable than sweeping claims. When you highlight a team that cut meeting time by 20% or an individual who gained confidence after one shift, people lean in because they can picture themselves in that story.

Another layer of proof is consistency over time. One great result might capture attention, but a pattern of results builds reputation. When people see you delivering outcomes month after month, year after year, your authority becomes almost unshakable. Longevity itself becomes proof.

And finally, proof invites participation. When your audience sees clear evidence of impact, they begin to imagine themselves as the next success story. Proof not only validates your message—it sparks belief in what's possible for others. That's when your authority moves from inspiration to transformation.

Day 43 is about weaving proof into your content. You don't have to oversell—just offer honest evidence that what you share makes a difference.

The story of Day 43 is this: proof transforms belief into trust. Without it, your authority feels hollow. With it, your influence solidifies.

Activity: Collect one piece of proof today—a story, testimonial, or result—that demonstrates the impact of your clarity.

Reflection: How does sharing proof shift the way others perceive your authority?

Day 44: Building Authority (Credibility & Multipliers)

Day 44 is about partnerships. Authority grows not only through your own voice but also through association with others. When you collaborate with credible people, their trust extends to you, and your authority multiplies.

I once partnered with a respected leader on a small project. My audience saw me differently afterward—not because I changed, but because the association elevated my credibility. Partnerships amplify authority through shared trust.

Partnerships don't have to be grand. They can be as simple as co-hosting a webinar, writing an article together, or even having conversations that are visible to your audience. The key is intentionality—choose partners whose values align with yours.

The danger is chasing partnerships for status rather than alignment. If you collaborate with people who don't reflect your values, their credibility won't amplify yours—it will erode it.

Day 44 is about being strategic and authentic with partnerships. Look for collaborations that create mutual value and strengthen your shared message.

The story of Day 44 is this: partnerships multiply clarity when they're built on trust and alignment. Choose them wisely.

Activity: Identify one person you admire whose values align with yours. Brainstorm a small way to collaborate with them this month.

Reflection: How could this partnership amplify your clarity and credibility?

Day 45: Building Authority (Credibility & Multipliers)

Day 45 is about multiplication. Authority compounds when you stop thinking of it as a solo project and start seeing it as something to be multiplied through others. When you empower others to carry your message, your influence expands beyond your own efforts.

I once worked with a leader who insisted on doing everything herself. Her reach stayed small because her authority stopped at the edge of her own energy. When she began training others to share her methods, her impact multiplied.

Multiplication requires trust. It means releasing control and allowing others to interpret and carry your message. It's not about cloning yourself—it's about equipping others to add their own voice to the clarity you've built.

The beauty of multiplication is that it creates momentum. The more people carry your message, the more credible and powerful it becomes. Authority grows exponentially when it's shared.

Multiplication also creates resilience. When your clarity depends only on you, it's fragile—one setback, illness, or shift in priorities can stall it. But when others are carrying pieces of your vision, your message can keep moving even when you pause. Shared clarity outlives individual capacity.

I've seen communities transform when leaders make this shift. Instead of one voice holding the spotlight, a chorus emerges. Each person amplifies the message in their own context, reaching audiences the original leader could never touch. Multiplication extends both breadth and depth.

And here's the deeper reward: multiplication is how influence becomes legacy. Your clarity stops being tied to your calendar and starts taking on a life of its own. When others carry it forward in their own ways, you've moved from building impact to planting seeds that can grow for generations.

Multiplication ultimately asks a simple question: do you want to be impressive, or do you want to be impactful? Impressive moments fade when the spotlight moves on, but impact multiplies when others carry your clarity into spaces you'll never enter. Choosing multiplication is choosing to matter beyond yourself.

Day 45 is about moving from ownership to stewardship. Your clarity isn't meant to stay locked within you—it's meant to multiply through others.

The story of Day 45 is this: authority that multiplies becomes legacy. When others carry your clarity forward, your influence outlives your effort.

Activity: Identify one way you could equip someone else to carry part of your message—through mentoring, resources, or collaboration.

Reflection: How does sharing authority multiply your impact beyond what you can do alone?

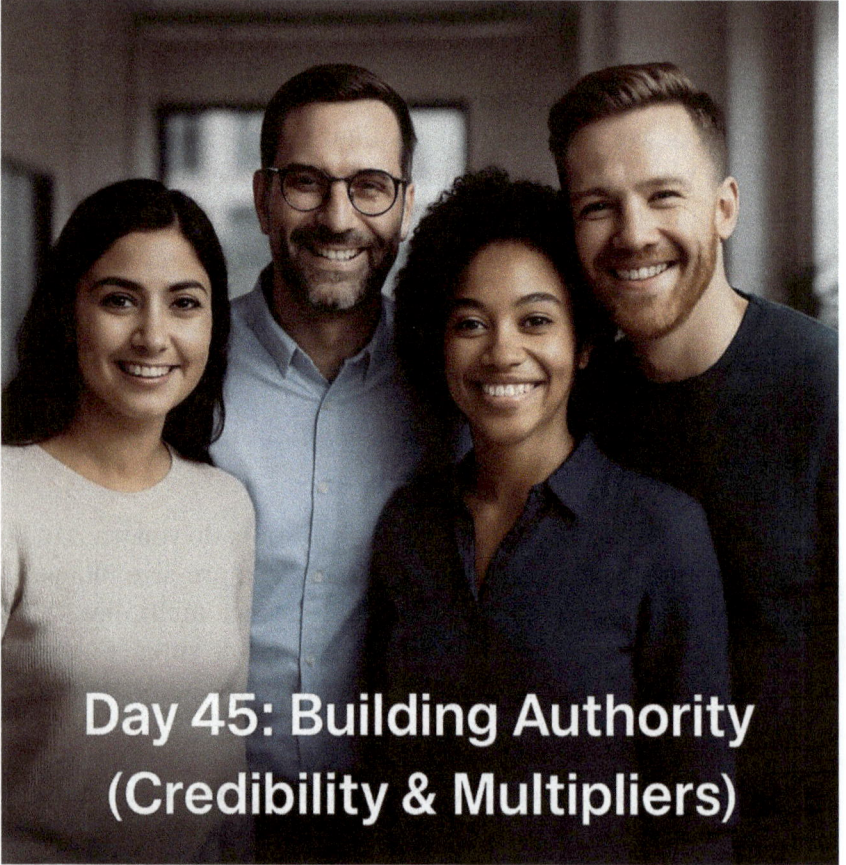
Day 45: Building Authority
(Credibility & Multipliers)

Day 46: Building Authority (Proof & Trust in Action)

Day 46 is about social proof. Authority isn't only what you say about yourself—it's what others say about you. When your audience hears stories of people who have benefited from your clarity, trust grows naturally.

I once coached a consultant who hesitated to ask clients for testimonials. She worried it felt pushy. But when she finally gathered them, she realized the power wasn't in her words—it was in their voices. Her audience trusted her more because the proof came from others.

Social proof doesn't have to be elaborate. A simple story, a quote from someone you helped, or a short endorsement can go further than a polished pitch.

The truth is, we all look for evidence before we trust. Social proof provides that evidence in a way that feels authentic and believable.

Day 46 is about recognizing that authority multiplies when others carry your message. Their stories become your proof.

The story of Day 46 is this: social proof turns credibility into community. When others share their trust, your clarity expands further than it could alone.

Activity: Ask one client, colleague, or friend to share a short story of how you've impacted them. Capture it as social proof.

Reflection: How does hearing your impact through someone else's words shift your sense of authority?

Day 47: Building Authority (Proof & Trust in Action)

Day 47 is about visibility. Authority requires being seen. You could be brilliant, but if no one knows you exist, your clarity can't spread. Visibility isn't vanity—it's stewardship of your message.

I once knew a professional who had incredible insights but kept them hidden in private journals. When she began sharing publicly, her career transformed. Opportunities found her because people finally saw her clarity in action.

Visibility is about showing up in the spaces where your audience already spends time. It's not about chasing every platform—it's about choosing the right ones and being consistent there.

Fear often keeps people hidden. Fear of judgment, fear of failure, fear of being misunderstood. But the cost of hiding is greater than the cost of visibility. Without visibility, your clarity remains locked inside.

Day 47 is about courageously stepping into the light. Not to seek fame, but to serve. Visibility gives your message a chance to reach the people who need it most.

The story of Day 47 is this: clarity unseen is clarity unused. Visibility is how you multiply the impact of your genius.

Activity: Choose one platform or community where your audience is active. Share one piece of your clarity there this week.

Reflection: How does choosing visibility shift your confidence and opportunities?

Day 48: Building Authority (Proof & Trust in Action)

Day 48 is about trust. Authority doesn't grow from a single post or a single project—it grows from repeated trust deposits over time. Every interaction is either building or eroding trust.

I once hired a contractor who delivered on time, every time. Even when challenges arose, he communicated clearly. Over time, my trust in him became unshakable. His authority with me wasn't built in a day—it was built through consistent reliability.

Trust works the same way with your audience. They notice when you show up consistently. They notice when your message aligns with your actions. Over time, these small signals accumulate into authority.

The danger is underestimating the small moments. Missing deadlines, ignoring feedback, or disappearing without communication erodes trust faster than you think. Authority is fragile when trust is ignored.

Day 48 is about remembering that trust is your greatest currency. When people trust you, they follow you. When they don't, they forget you.

The story of Day 48 is this: authority is built at the speed of trust—and lost at the speed of doubt.

Activity: Identify one small trust-building action you can take today—replying to a message, meeting a deadline, or following up with someone.

Reflection: How does focusing on small trust deposits shift your sense of authority?

Day 49: Building Authority (Proof & Trust in Action)

Day 46 is about social proof. Authority isn't only what you say about yourself—it's what others say about you. When your audience hears stories of people who have benefited from your clarity, trust grows naturally.

I once coached a consultant who hesitated to ask clients for testimonials. She worried it felt pushy. But when she finally gathered them, she realized the power wasn't in her words—it was in their voices. Her audience trusted her more because the proof came from others.

Social proof doesn't have to be elaborate. A simple story, a quote from someone you helped, or a short endorsement can go further than a polished pitch.

The truth is, we all look for evidence before we trust. Social proof provides that evidence in a way that feels authentic and believable.

One of the most powerful aspects of social proof is relatability. When someone sees a story from a person "like them," the message resonates more deeply. It shifts from "That sounds inspiring" to "If they can do it, maybe I can too." This is why stories from peers or colleagues often carry more weight than statistics alone—they bridge the gap between possibility and reality.

Social proof also scales your influence. You can only speak so many words or write so many posts, but when others carry your message, the reach multiplies. Every testimonial, endorsement, or case study becomes another voice amplifying your clarity. In time, these voices build a chorus that speaks louder than you ever could on your own.

I've seen leaders transform when they stop fearing the ask. Gathering social proof isn't about self-promotion—it's about honoring the voices of those you've impacted. When you highlight their stories, you not only strengthen your credibility but also celebrate their growth. It becomes less about you and more about the community of change you're creating.

Social proof also builds resilience. When doubt creeps in, your own words may not convince you, but the reminders from those you've helped can anchor you. Their stories become evidence you can lean on, not just for your audience's trust, but for your own confidence in seasons of uncertainty.

And here's the deeper truth: social proof creates belonging. When others share their trust in you, it doesn't just validate your message—it builds a community around it. People no longer see themselves as isolated listeners; they become part of a movement shaped by clarity, trust, and shared experience.

Day 46 is about recognizing that authority multiplies when others carry your message. Their stories become your proof.

The story of Day 46 is this: social proof turns credibility into community. When others share their trust, your clarity expands further than it could alone.

Activity: Ask one client, colleague, or friend to share a short story of how you've impacted them. Capture it as social proof.

Reflection: How does hearing your impact through someone else's words shift your sense of authority?

Day 50: Building Authority (Proof & Trust in Action)

Day 50 is about generosity. Authority isn't built by hoarding knowledge—it's built by giving it away. When you share generously, people begin to see you as a trusted resource rather than a gatekeeper.

I once watched a leader share a free guide that others would have charged for. Instead of devaluing her expertise, it amplified it. People trusted her more because she gave first without demanding anything in return.

Generosity doesn't mean giving everything away. It means offering enough value that people know you are invested in their success, not just your own.

The paradox of generosity is that the more you give, the more you gain. Not because you're manipulating, but because trust grows when people feel seen and supported.

Day 50 is about shifting from scarcity to abundance. Scarcity says, 'Protect your knowledge or you'll lose power.' Abundance says, 'Share your knowledge and your power will multiply.'

The story of Day 50 is this: authority rooted in generosity creates legacy. People remember the leaders who gave, not the ones who withheld.

Activity: Share one resource, idea, or lesson today with no strings attached. Notice how it impacts the way others engage with you.

Reflection: How does generosity shift your perspective on building authority?

Where in your life or work are you tempted to hold back knowledge or resources?

What is one area where you could give more freely without fear of "losing" authority?

How has someone else's generosity impacted you, and how can you model that same spirit?

If you practiced generosity consistently for the next year, how might your influence, trust, and relationships shift?

[Write here]

_____

_____

_____

_____

Day 51: Action (Taking Clarity into Motion)

Day 51 is about momentum through small steps. Too often we think action has to be massive to matter. But clarity compounds when you take consistent small steps in the right direction.

I once worked with a client who dreamed of writing a book but felt paralyzed by the enormity of it. So we broke it down: write one paragraph a day. Within months, she had chapters. Within a year, a full draft. Her book wasn't born from a single leap but from hundreds of small, steady steps.

Small actions are underestimated because they don't feel dramatic. But the truth is, they're sustainable. Dramatic bursts often fade, while small steps build momentum that lasts.

Clarity doesn't demand heroics. It demands faithfulness. Each step you take reinforces your identity as someone moving forward.

Day 51 is about rejecting paralysis by scale. You don't need to do everything today. You just need to take the next clear step.

I've seen leaders unlock breakthroughs by embracing this mindset. One manager reduced a team's reporting backlog not by overhauling the system overnight, but by asking each team member to resolve just one issue daily. Within weeks, the backlog had shrunk dramatically. What seemed impossible began to feel inevitable because the weight of progress shifted through small, steady actions.

The beauty of small steps is that they create a feedback loop. Each completed step builds confidence, and that confidence fuels the next action. Over time, the momentum becomes self-sustaining. What once felt overwhelming now feels natural, even energizing. You no longer dread the mountain—you focus on the next foothold.

There's also a hidden power in celebrating small wins. Too often we dismiss them as insignificant. But when you pause to acknowledge progress, you reinforce the behavior. A single step might not finish the journey, but it strengthens your identity as someone who moves forward, no matter how slowly.

Small steps also help us recover from setbacks. Life will inevitably bring interruptions, delays, or failures. When your progress is built on dramatic bursts, setbacks can feel catastrophic. But when it's built on small steps, recovery is easier. You simply pick up the next step again. Momentum may slow, but it never dies.

And here's the paradox: small steps often lead to big leaps. By showing up consistently, you create opportunities that would never have appeared otherwise. The client who wrote a paragraph a day didn't just finish a book—she attracted speaking opportunities, collaborations, and a platform she never imagined. None of it came from waiting for the perfect moment—it all came from small steps taken consistently.

Small steps also reframe your relationship with time. Instead of fearing long timelines, you learn to trust the compounding effect of steady progress. What seems distant becomes attainable when you realize each day's effort is an investment in the future.

They also cultivate patience. In a world obsessed with instant results, choosing to build through small steps trains you to value process over speed. This patience not only preserves your energy— it often produces deeper, more lasting results.

Another gift of small steps is accessibility. Anyone can take them, regardless of resources, status, or circumstances. Small steps democratize progress; they remind us that clarity is not reserved for the privileged few but available to anyone willing to begin.

Finally, small steps anchor you in the present. Instead of being crushed by the weight of the entire journey, you learn to focus on what's right in front of you. That presence brings peace, because you no longer carry tomorrow's worries while you walk today's path.

The story of Day 51 is this: small steps create big clarity. The momentum of action matters more than the size of action.

Activity: Choose one goal you've been delaying. Break it down into the smallest possible step and take it today.

Reflection: How does taking one small step shift your energy and confidence?

Day 52: Action (Taking Clarity into Motion)

Day 52 is about imperfection. Many people delay action because they want everything to be flawless. But clarity grows when you're willing to act imperfectly.

I once knew a leader who wouldn't launch a project until every detail was polished. As a result, he missed opportunities and burned out his team. When he finally embraced imperfection, his work multiplied in impact because it actually reached people.

Perfectionism masquerades as excellence, but it's really fear in disguise. It keeps you from moving forward because nothing ever feels 'ready enough.'

The truth is, imperfect action beats perfect inaction every time. The world doesn't need perfect—it needs progress. And progress only happens through action.

Day 52 is about letting go of the illusion of perfect timing and flawless execution. What matters is that you move, even if it's messy.

The story of Day 52 is this: imperfect action creates clarity. Each attempt teaches you more than endless planning ever could.

Activity: Take one action today you've been avoiding because it feels imperfect. Do it anyway, and note what you learn.

Reflection: How does embracing imperfection shift your relationship with clarity and progress?

Day 53: Action (Taking Clarity into Motion)

Day 53 is about courage in visibility. It's one thing to plan and prepare, but action requires stepping into view. Clarity becomes powerful when others can see it.

I once worked with an entrepreneur who had built a brilliant system but kept it hidden in spreadsheets on her computer. When she finally shared it in a workshop, people were amazed—and opportunities poured in. Her clarity only mattered because she made it visible.

Visibility is vulnerable. It means risking criticism or misunderstanding. But it also means inviting impact. You can't change lives from the shadows.

Every leader I admire reached influence not because they were the smartest but because they were brave enough to be seen. Action in public multiplies clarity far more than quiet preparation ever can.

Day 53 is about showing up where others can experience your clarity. Not to prove yourself, but to serve.

I've learned that visibility also requires resilience. When you step forward, not everyone will applaud. Some will critique, misunderstand, or even dismiss what you offer. But courage in visibility means valuing impact over approval. If your clarity helps even one person, the risk was worth it.

Visibility also has a compounding effect. The first time you share, it feels terrifying. The tenth time, it feels natural. Each act of visibility strengthens your confidence and expands your reach. What once felt like a leap becomes part of your rhythm, and clarity flows more freely.

And here's the paradox: the very things you fear might make you look weak are often the things that make you most relatable. Sharing an unfinished idea, a personal failure, or a behind-the-scenes struggle creates connection. People trust you more because you've chosen to be real instead of polished.

I've seen teams transform when leaders practice visibility. When leaders openly communicate progress, struggles, and next steps, the team feels included and empowered. Hidden clarity creates confusion; visible clarity creates alignment.

Visibility is also an act of stewardship. Your ideas, gifts, and clarity are not just for you—they're for others. Keeping them hidden robs the world of the impact they could have. Sharing them honors both your genius and the people waiting to benefit from it.

Finally, visibility reminds us that leadership isn't about control—it's about contribution. You don't have to know how far your clarity will reach. You just have to be willing to release it into the world.

Once it's visible, it takes on a life of its own, multiplying impact in ways you may never fully see.

The story of Day 53 is this: clarity hidden is clarity wasted. Visibility turns action into impact.

Activity: Share one piece of your work publicly today, even if it feels vulnerable. It could be a post, a story, or an idea.

Reflection: What shifts when your clarity moves from private to public action?

Day 54: Action (Taking Clarity into Motion)

Day 54 is about resilience. Action is not a straight line. You will face setbacks, criticism, and failure along the way. The key is learning to keep moving even when the path feels rough.

I once led a project that failed publicly. For weeks I felt crushed, convinced it had ruined my credibility. But as I processed it, I realized the failure became my teacher. I learned more from that one setback than from a dozen successes.

Resilience doesn't mean you enjoy failure. It means you don't let it define you. Each setback becomes a stepping stone when you frame it as part of the journey.

Your clarity isn't fragile—it can withstand failure. In fact, failure often sharpens it. The question is not, 'Will I fail?' but 'How will I respond when I do?'

Day 54 is about embracing resilience as part of action. Progress isn't about avoiding bumps—it's about learning to keep moving through them.

The story of Day 54 is this: resilience turns setbacks into strength. Action rooted in resilience compounds over time.

Activity: Write about one failure you've experienced. Identify at least one lesson it gave you that now supports your clarity.

Reflection: How does reframing failure as a teacher shift your willingness to act again?

Day 55: Action (Taking Clarity into Motion)

Day 55 is about momentum through community. Taking action alone is powerful, but taking action together is exponential. When you act alongside others, you gain accountability, encouragement, and shared energy.

I once joined a small mastermind group where we each committed to weekly actions. Knowing I had to report back pushed me to follow through. And hearing their progress inspired me to keep moving.

Community multiplies courage. When you see others acting, it reminds you that you can too. Their momentum fuels yours, and your momentum fuels theirs.

The danger of isolation is that setbacks feel heavier and wins feel smaller. In community, setbacks feel lighter and wins feel worth celebrating.

Day 55 is about choosing not to act alone. Find people who are also moving forward, and let their momentum help carry you.

The story of Day 55 is this: action grows stronger in community. Together, clarity accelerates.

Activity: Find one person or group to share your next action step with. Commit together to hold each other accountable.

Reflection: How does community change the way you approach taking action?

Day 56: Action (Sustaining & Scaling Clarity)

Day 56 is about discipline. Momentum begins with small steps, but sustaining it requires discipline. Discipline is the quiet engine behind every visible success.

I once admired a speaker who seemed effortlessly charismatic. Later, I learned his secret wasn't talent—it was discipline. He practiced daily, refined his craft, and treated preparation like sacred work. His clarity wasn't luck. It was discipline over time.

Discipline doesn't mean rigidity. It means showing up even when inspiration is absent. It's choosing the long-term benefit of clarity over the short-term comfort of excuses.

Without discipline, clarity flickers in and out. With discipline, it becomes steady, reliable, and trustworthy. People don't follow brilliance that's occasional—they follow consistency that's disciplined.

Day 56 is about embracing discipline as a gift, not a burden. It's what makes your clarity sustainable instead of fleeting.

The story of Day 56 is this: discipline fuels clarity. The more you honor the practice, the brighter the light shines.

Activity: Identify one area of your journey that needs more discipline. Commit to one small habit that strengthens it this week.

Reflection: How does practicing discipline change your confidence in sustaining clarity?

Day 57: Action (Sustaining & Scaling Clarity)

Day 57 is about systems. Action sustained over time requires more than willpower—it requires systems that make consistency easier.

I once worked with a leader who was brilliant but constantly overwhelmed. His ideas were strong, but his lack of systems made his clarity scatter. Once he built a simple process for managing tasks, his creativity and focus skyrocketed.

Systems aren't glamorous, but they are what free you to focus on what matters most. A strong system takes the weight off your mind and gives clarity room to grow.

The best systems are simple. A calendar that you actually use. A checklist you trust. A workflow that reduces friction. Complexity kills systems—simplicity sustains them.

Day 57 is about building systems that support your genius. You don't need the perfect tool—you need a reliable process.

Systems also create accountability. When you can see your commitments clearly laid out, you're less likely to forget them or let them slide. They provide an external structure that supports the promises you've made to yourself and to others.

They also make delegation possible. Without systems, you're the bottleneck—everything depends on your memory or effort. With systems, you can hand off tasks with confidence, knowing the process will guide others just as it guides you.

And systems bring peace. Chaos thrives in uncertainty, but order creates calm. When you know there's a place for every task, every idea, every responsibility, your mind no longer has to carry the burden. That calm becomes fertile ground for clarity and creativity.

The story of Day 57 is this: systems protect clarity. They turn discipline into something sustainable and scalable.

Activity: Review one area of your life or work that feels chaotic. Build or refine a simple system to support it.

Reflection: How does creating systems free up your energy for clarity and creativity?

Day 58: Action (Sustaining & Scaling Clarity)

Day 58 is about alignment. Sustained clarity requires that your actions match your values and vision. Misalignment slowly erodes clarity until momentum disappears.

I once knew a business owner whose company was profitable but draining. He realized his actions no longer aligned with his values. When he adjusted his strategy to reflect his deeper purpose, his energy returned—and so did his clarity.

Alignment is not static. It requires regular check-ins: Does this path still serve my vision? Does this work reflect my genius? Without alignment, even success feels empty.

The gift of alignment is energy. When your actions match your values, you feel lighter, stronger, more focused. Clarity becomes effortless because you're no longer fighting yourself.

Day 58 is about treating alignment as a practice. The clearer you are on your values, the easier it is to sustain clarity over time.

I've seen leaders rediscover their drive simply by realigning one area of their lives. For some, it meant shifting from endless travel to more time at home. For others, it meant choosing clients and projects that matched their mission instead of just their revenue goals. Small adjustments in alignment often create outsized gains in energy.

Misalignment, on the other hand, leaves clues: constant fatigue, resentment, or a nagging sense of "this isn't it." These signals aren't failures—they're invitations to course-correct. Paying attention to them is part of the work of clarity.

And alignment creates integrity. When your words, choices, and actions all line up, people trust you more deeply. That trust strengthens your influence, but more importantly, it frees you from the exhausting work of pretending. Alignment allows you to show up whole.

The story of Day 58 is this: alignment fuels longevity. Without it, clarity fades. With it, clarity compounds.

Activity: Write down your top three values. Reflect on whether your current actions align with them, and adjust one area where they don't.

Reflection: How does realignment restore your sense of clarity and energy?

中

Day 59: Action (Sustaining & Scaling Clarity)

Day 59 is about renewal. Even with discipline, systems, and alignment, you cannot sustain clarity without rest. Renewal is what refuels the engine so you can keep moving forward.

I once burned out from overwork, convinced that rest was a luxury I couldn't afford. The result was months of exhaustion that slowed my progress more than rest ever would have. Renewal isn't optional—it's essential.

Renewal looks different for everyone. For some, it's solitude. For others, connection. For some, creativity. The key is knowing what restores you and making it part of your rhythm.

Without renewal, clarity turns to burnout. With renewal, clarity becomes sustainable joy.

Day 59 is about rejecting the lie that constant hustle builds success. True clarity thrives on a rhythm of work and renewal.

I've seen leaders discover that renewal often creates their breakthroughs. A pause in nature, an afternoon off, or even a quiet weekend away has sparked solutions they couldn't force during long hours at their desk. Renewal doesn't take you away from clarity—it returns you to it sharper, fresher, and more focused.

Renewal also strengthens resilience. Life and leadership will always bring setbacks, but when your tank is full, you can absorb challenges without collapsing. Rest creates a margin of strength that hustle alone can never provide. Renewal is not indulgence—it is preparation.

The hardest part of renewal is often permission. Many of us carry guilt when we rest, as if stopping makes us lazy or irresponsible. But renewal is not neglect—it is stewardship. You can't lead others to clarity if you're running on fumes. Giving yourself permission to rest is one of the most courageous acts of leadership.

I've noticed, too, that renewal can be contagious. When a leader models healthy rhythms, others in their orbit feel free to do the same. A team that sees its leader rest without apology will learn that they, too, are valued for their clarity, not just their output. Renewal becomes a cultural practice, not just a personal choice.

And finally, renewal reconnects us with joy. Work done without rest eventually feels heavy, even when it's meaningful. But when you weave in rhythms of renewal, you return to your work with gratitude, energy, and passion. Renewal doesn't just sustain clarity—it restores the joy of pursuing it.

The story of Day 59 is this: renewal is not weakness—it's wisdom. Rest sustains clarity more than endless effort ever could.

Activity: Plan one intentional act of renewal this week—time off, creative play, or connection with loved ones.

Reflection: How does renewal strengthen your ability to sustain clarity over the long haul?

Day 60: Action (Sustaining & Scaling Clarity)

Day 60 is about scaling. After 30 days of clarity in Part I and 30 days of action in Part II, you are ready to think bigger. Scaling doesn't mean doing more for the sake of more—it means multiplying impact while staying aligned.

I once worked with a nonprofit leader who grew her impact not by working harder but by equipping others to carry the vision with her. She scaled not through addition but through multiplication.

Scaling requires asking: how can I extend my clarity to more people without losing its essence? That might mean teaching, mentoring, automating, or delegating. Scaling happens when you build structures that carry your clarity beyond your direct reach.

The danger is scaling without sustainability. If growth outpaces systems, alignment, or renewal, clarity collapses. True scaling balances growth with strength.

Day 60 is about envisioning the next level. It's not about chasing bigger numbers—it's about expanding your impact in ways that stay true to your genius and your values.

Scaling also requires simplicity. The clearer and simpler your message, the easier it is for others to carry it. Complexity doesn't multiply well. What multiplies are ideas and practices that can be remembered, repeated, and lived out by others.

Another key to scaling is stewardship. You are not just growing for your own success—you are creating opportunities for others to thrive. When you scale well, you're not only extending your reach, you're empowering others to step into their own clarity.

I've seen leaders attempt to scale by clinging to control. Instead of multiplying, they micromanaged, and growth stalled. Real scaling requires releasing—not hoarding—authority. The more you empower others, the more the vision grows beyond what you could do alone.

Scaling also brings new responsibility. The greater your influence, the more intentional you must be about alignment, values, and integrity. Impact multiplies both your strengths and your weaknesses, so scaling requires vigilance as much as ambition.

And here's the gift: scaling isn't about ego—it's about legacy. When your clarity outlives your direct involvement, you know you've built something that matters. Scaling transforms your work from personal success into lasting significance.

The story of Day 60 is this: scaling clarity creates legacy. It's how your light continues to shine beyond you.

Activity: Identify one way you can scale your clarity—through teaching, delegating, or creating a resource others can use.

Reflection: How does scaling your clarity expand your sense of purpose and possibility?

Where in your life or work do you sense it's time to think bigger?

What part of your clarity is simple enough to be multiplied through others?

Who could you teach, mentor, or equip to carry your message forward?

What systems or safeguards will you need to keep scaling sustainable?

How would scaling shift your sense of purpose from success to legacy?

[Write here]

_____

_____

_____

_____

Part III – Applying Clarity to Life & Leadership

Here we move beyond practice into real-world application. You'll explore how to bring clarity into your business leadership, your role in your community, and even your family life. Clarity is not confined to one space—it's a way of living.

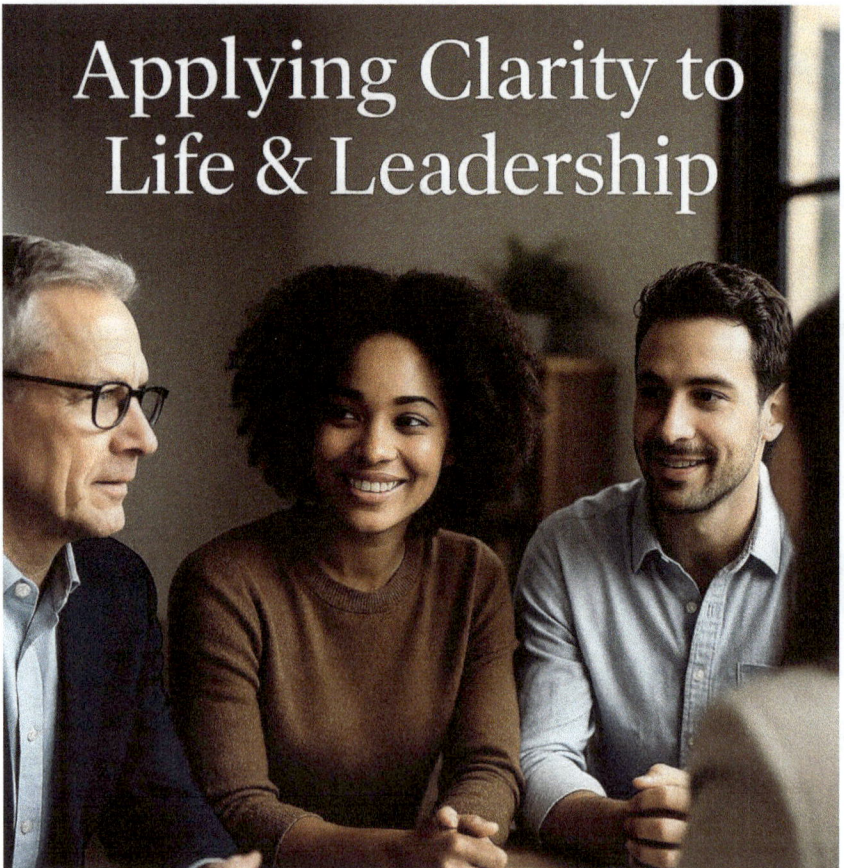

Applying Clarity to Life & Leadership

Day 61: Applying Thought Leadership in Business Teams

Trust is In many organizations, influence doesn't come from titles alone—it comes from clarity. I once worked with a mid-level manager who had no formal authority, yet he became the person everyone turned to when problems grew complex. His secret wasn't power; it was perspective.

When challenges arose, he didn't rush to offer solutions. Instead, he asked questions that revealed what the team had overlooked. By slowing the conversation down, he helped people see the real issue instead of circling symptoms. His clarity cut through confusion like a signal in static.

The remarkable part was that he never demanded attention. He didn't raise his voice or push his agenda. His leadership emerged quietly, in the way he reframed discussions and invited others to contribute. That humility made his influence even stronger.

Many people think leadership must come from the top of the org chart. But thought leadership proves otherwise. Anyone can shape the direction of a team when they consistently bring clarity, honesty, and a collaborative spirit.

This manager's approach showed me that teams don't need more noise—they need someone willing to create space for understanding. By clarifying, not commanding, he inspired trust. People sought him out not because he had authority, but because he brought perspective.

Teams thrive when someone provides that kind of anchor. Without it, meetings drag, projects stall, and energy drains. With it, momentum builds. People leave conversations knowing what matters most and how to move forward.

Thought leadership in teams is about presence, not position. It's choosing to guide through insight rather than control. The power is not in answering every question but in asking the right ones at the right time.

As I watched this manager work, I realized that clarity is contagious. Once he modeled it, others began framing their ideas more thoughtfully too. His quiet leadership raised the standard of the whole group.

What this story shows is that leadership is often less about authority and more about courage—the courage to slow down, to listen, and to bring a sharper lens to shared problems. That kind of clarity strengthens the whole team.

Trust is built when people know what to expect from you. This manager became a steady presence—the kind of person who didn't waver with pressure or politics. That consistency gave his colleagues confidence, because they knew his perspective wasn't swayed by ego or fear but by a genuine desire for clarity.

Another lesson I learned from watching him was that clarity requires restraint. It's tempting to jump in with answers, especially when tensions run high. But by holding back and asking the right questions, he helped the group own the solution together. That restraint created buy-in far stronger than if he had simply dictated a path forward.

Clarity also works like a compass in conflict. In heated debates, people often argue past each other without realizing they're solving different problems. A clarifying voice can pause the room and ask, "What are we really trying to solve here?" That simple question reorients the team and prevents wasted energy.

The influence of clarity stretches beyond meetings. It shapes culture. Over time, a team that learns to value clarity becomes less reactive and more thoughtful. Decisions improve, relationships strengthen, and trust deepens—not because someone took control, but because someone set a different tone.

Clarity-driven leadership also makes space for others to grow. By creating an environment where people feel heard and guided rather than controlled, you empower them to develop their own clarity. In this way, trust multiplies as others step into the same posture of thoughtful leadership.

And perhaps most importantly, clarity builds credibility. Titles may open doors, but trust keeps them open. When people experience you as the person who makes things clearer, you become the voice they seek when it matters most. That is influence no title can grant and no hierarchy can contain.

Your clarity can do the same. Even if you're not the official leader, you can become the trusted voice others rely on to navigate challenges and opportunities together.

Activity: Identify one meeting this week where you can bring clarity by framing the problem or asking a clarifying question.

Reflection: How does shifting from problem-solving to clarity-sharing change the way your team responds to you?

Day 62: Applying Thought Leadership in Business Teams

Trust is the soil where thought leadership grows. Without it, even the sharpest insights fail to take root. I once watched two leaders at the same company—one with impressive strategies that never gained traction, the other with ordinary ideas that carried enormous weight.

The difference wasn't talent. It was trust. The trusted leader showed up consistently. She remembered small details about people's lives. She followed through on commitments. Over time, her team believed in her not just because of her words, but because of her reliability.

Meanwhile, the other leader dazzled with ideas but often missed deadlines or dismissed input. His brilliance was undermined by inconsistency. The team learned not to rely on him, and his authority dwindled.

Trust is built in moments so small they're easy to overlook—returning a call when you said you would, admitting when you don't know, listening without judgment. Each act is like a deposit in a bank account of credibility.

When teams know they can depend on you, they lean into your leadership. Even difficult truths land more softly when trust is strong, because people know your intent is to help, not to harm.

But trust cannot be rushed. It grows slowly, like roots beneath the surface, unseen but essential. Break it once, and it takes ten times the effort to repair. That's why consistency matters as much as clarity.

Thought leadership without trust feels hollow. People may nod politely, but they won't act on what you share. When trust is present, even a modest suggestion can spark momentum.

The leader who invested in trust built influence that outlasted projects and job titles. Her team carried her lessons forward because they trusted the source.

What this shows is that clarity may open the door, but trust keeps it open. Together, they create the foundation for sustainable leadership inside any team.

You don't need to be brilliant to lead with thought—just trustworthy. Build trust daily, and your clarity will find its place.

Activity: Find one small promise you can make to your team today—and keep it. Notice how follow-through builds credibility.

Reflection: How does keeping small promises shift the way your team sees your leadership?

Day 63: Applying Thought Leadership in Business Teams

Every team faces conflict. The difference between thriving and dysfunctional groups is not whether conflict happens—it's how it's handled. I once worked with a team that avoided conflict at all costs. Meetings were quiet, polite, and unproductive. Beneath the surface, resentment grew.

Avoiding conflict didn't protect the team—it poisoned it. People stopped speaking up, decisions were half-hearted, and innovation died. Silence became the enemy of progress.

Contrast that with another team I observed where disagreements were common but healthy. They didn't fear tension; they framed it as opportunity. When perspectives clashed, they leaned in instead of pulling away.

One manager in that group developed a simple habit. Whenever debates got heated, she said, "It sounds like we see this differently—

let's explore why." That one phrase shifted the tone from defensive to curious.

With that approach, arguments became discoveries. People realized they weren't enemies—they were allies uncovering better answers together. Disagreement stopped being a threat and became a tool.

Conflict, reframed, sharpened their focus. Instead of circling vague frustrations, they clarified assumptions and found solutions faster. The very thing they once avoided became their strength.

This is the essence of thought leadership in teams: not eliminating discomfort, but guiding it toward clarity. By stepping into conflict with curiosity, leaders model how to transform tension into trust.

Over time, this culture of curiosity built resilience. The team grew more confident in facing challenges, knowing that friction didn't mean failure—it meant growth was near.

What this story shows is that conflict is not the opposite of clarity— it is often the path to it. Leaders who reframe conflict open doors to understanding that avoidance keeps locked.

When your team faces conflict, remember: the goal is not to win the argument, but to find the clarity that lies beneath the noise.

Activity: The next time conflict arises, ask a clarifying question instead of shutting it down. Practice curiosity instead of defensiveness.

Reflection: How does reframing conflict as an opportunity change the way your team navigates it?

Day 64: Applying Thought Leadership in Business Teams

Vision gives teams direction. Without it, they drift. With it, they move with purpose. I once saw a leader draft a vision statement alone and present it to the team with fanfare. It sounded inspiring but fell flat. No one owned it because no one helped create it.

In another organization, a leader tried a different approach. She brought her team together for a workshop, asking them to describe what success would look like in their own words. The resulting vision was imperfect in grammar but powerful in ownership.

Because the team co-created it, they remembered it. They reminded each other of it in tough moments. The vision became more than words on a wall—it became a compass in daily decisions.

Thought leadership here meant guiding the process, not dictating the outcome. The leader resisted the urge to control and instead created space for the team's collective clarity to emerge.

That choice paid off. Motivation shifted from compliance to commitment. People weren't just following instructions—they were pursuing a shared purpose they believed in.

Vision doesn't have to be grand to work. It has to be clear, relevant, and owned. A single sentence that everyone remembers beats a polished paragraph that no one believes.

When leaders open the floor, they uncover perspectives that sharpen the vision. Diversity of thought turns vague aspirations into grounded direction.

The process itself becomes a trust-builder. Teams see that their voice matters, and that makes them more invested in the journey ahead.

What this story shows is that vision imposed from above is decoration. Vision created together is direction. Leaders who invite contribution multiply ownership.

Your role is not to hand your team a map—it's to help them draw it, so they'll be eager to walk the path.

Activity: Facilitate a conversation with your team about your shared purpose. Capture their words instead of writing it for them.

Reflection: How does inviting your team into vision-shaping shift their energy and engagement?

Day 65: Applying Thought Leadership in Business Teams

Feedback is fuel for growth. But too often, teams treat it as a one-way street—managers giving, employees receiving. True thought leadership flips that. It creates a culture where feedback flows freely in every direction.

I once saw a leader who constantly asked for feedback but bristled whenever it came. His defensiveness silenced his team. Slowly, people stopped offering input, and the culture of improvement withered.

In contrast, another leader modeled gratitude. Whenever she received feedback—even criticism—she thanked the person first. That simple act made it safe for others to speak honestly.

Her openness shifted the whole team. Instead of fearing judgment, they embraced learning. Conversations grew sharper, faster, and more productive. Blind spots shrank because people were brave enough to point them out.

Feedback exposes what we cannot see alone. It turns fog into focus. Without it, teams wander in half-light. With it, they move in confidence.

But for feedback to work, it must feel safe. Safety comes from leaders who receive without retaliation and who model humility in practice.

When feedback is welcomed, it spreads. Teams stop hiding problems and start solving them. That courage accelerates growth far beyond what one person could drive alone.

The leader who modeled gratitude taught her team that learning beats perfection. Over time, that mindset built resilience and adaptability across the group.

What this story shows is that feedback is not weakness—it is wisdom. Leaders who embrace it create teams that evolve quickly and thrive under pressure.

Clarity grows fastest in cultures where feedback is welcomed as a gift, not feared as a weapon. Thought leadership makes that shift possible.

Activity: Ask your team for one piece of feedback on how you can lead better. Receive it without defense, and thank them for it.

Reflection: How does welcoming feedback instead of resisting it change the culture of your team?

Day 66: Applying Thought Leadership in Business Teams

Delegation is often misunderstood. Many think it's about giving away tasks you don't want to do. But in teams, effective delegation is about trust and growth. A thought leader doesn't just hand off work—they empower others to step into clarity.

I once worked with a project leader who refused to delegate. She believed no one could meet her standards. The result was exhaustion for her and frustration for her team, who felt underutilized and undervalued.

Contrast that with another leader who viewed delegation as development. When she passed on responsibilities, she didn't disappear—she offered guidance and space. Her team members flourished, and she created a bench of capable leaders around her.

Delegation done well builds confidence in both directions. The leader learns to trust others, and the team learns to trust themselves. It multiplies capacity rather than draining it.

At its core, delegation is about stewardship, not control. It says, "I believe in you enough to trust you with this responsibility." That kind of trust transforms teams.

But delegation is not abdication. It requires clarity—clear expectations, clear outcomes, and clear support. Without clarity, delegation creates chaos instead of growth.

The teams that thrive are those where responsibility is shared, not hoarded. Thought leadership shines here by recognizing potential in others and nurturing it through meaningful opportunities.

Delegation is also about humility. It means letting go of the illusion that one person must carry it all. It acknowledges that leadership is stronger when shared.

What this shows is that delegation is not weakness—it's wisdom. Leaders who delegate well extend their influence far beyond what they could manage alone.

When you empower others, you multiply clarity. The more you delegate with purpose, the stronger your team becomes.

Delegation also creates resilience. When skills and responsibilities are spread across a team, the work doesn't collapse if one person is absent or transitions out. Shared responsibility ensures continuity, protecting both the team and the mission.

It also fosters ownership. People rise to the level of trust placed in them. When team members know they are not just completing tasks but carrying real responsibility, they approach their work with greater care, creativity, and accountability.

And perhaps most importantly, delegation develops future leaders. Every time you entrust someone with meaningful responsibility, you're not just completing today's work—you're preparing tomorrow's leadership. That's how clarity grows beyond a single individual and becomes a legacy.

Activity: Choose one responsibility you normally hold tightly. Delegate it to someone this week with clear guidance and support.

Reflection: How does entrusting responsibility to others expand your team's capacity and your leadership impact?

Day 67: Applying Thought Leadership in Business Teams

Trust is In many organizations, influence doesn't come from titles alone—it comes from clarity. I once worked with a mid-level manager who had no formal authority, yet he became the person everyone turned to when problems grew complex. His secret wasn't power; it was perspective.

When challenges arose, he didn't rush to offer solutions. Instead, he asked questions that revealed what the team had overlooked. By slowing the conversation down, he helped people see the real issue instead of circling symptoms. His clarity cut through confusion like a signal in static.

The remarkable part was that he never demanded attention. He didn't raise his voice or push his agenda. His leadership emerged quietly, in the way he reframed discussions and invited others to contribute. That humility made his influence even stronger.

Many people think leadership must come from the top of the org chart. But thought leadership proves otherwise. Anyone can shape the direction of a team when they consistently bring clarity, honesty, and a collaborative spirit.

This manager's approach showed me that teams don't need more noise—they need someone willing to create space for understanding. By clarifying, not commanding, he inspired trust. People sought him out not because he had authority, but because he brought perspective.

Teams thrive when someone provides that kind of anchor. Without it, meetings drag, projects stall, and energy drains. With it, momentum builds. People leave conversations knowing what matters most and how to move forward.

Thought leadership in teams is about presence, not position. It's choosing to guide through insight rather than control. The power is not in answering every question but in asking the right ones at the right time.

As I watched this manager work, I realized that clarity is contagious. Once he modeled it, others began framing their ideas more thoughtfully too. His quiet leadership raised the standard of the whole group.

What this story shows is that leadership is often less about authority and more about courage—the courage to slow down, to listen, and to bring a sharper lens to shared problems. That kind of clarity strengthens the whole team.

Trust is built when people know what to expect from you. This manager became a steady presence—the kind of person who didn't waver with pressure or politics. That consistency gave his colleagues confidence, because they knew his perspective wasn't swayed by ego or fear but by a genuine desire for clarity.

Another lesson I learned from watching him was that clarity requires restraint. It's tempting to jump in with answers, especially when tensions run high. But by holding back and asking the right questions, he helped the group own the solution together. That restraint created buy-in far stronger than if he had simply dictated a path forward.

Clarity also works like a compass in conflict. In heated debates, people often argue past each other without realizing they're solving different problems. A clarifying voice can pause the room and ask, "What are we really trying to solve here?" That simple question reorients the team and prevents wasted energy.

The influence of clarity stretches beyond meetings. It shapes culture. Over time, a team that learns to value clarity becomes less reactive and more thoughtful. Decisions improve, relationships strengthen, and trust deepens—not because someone took control, but because someone set a different tone.

Clarity-driven leadership also makes space for others to grow. By creating an environment where people feel heard and guided rather than controlled, you empower them to develop their own clarity. In this way, trust multiplies as others step into the same posture of thoughtful leadership.

And perhaps most importantly, clarity builds credibility. Titles may open doors, but trust keeps them open. When people experience you as the person who makes things clearer, you become the voice they seek when it matters most. That is influence no title can grant and no hierarchy can contain.

Your clarity can do the same. Even if you're not the official leader, you can become the trusted voice others rely on to navigate challenges and opportunities together.

Activity: Identify one meeting this week where you can bring clarity by framing the problem or asking a clarifying question.

Reflection: How does shifting from problem-solving to clarity-sharing change the way your team responds to you?

Building Trust Through Teamwork

Day 68: Applying Thought Leadership in Business Teams

Decision-making is a daily reality in business teams. Yet many teams stall not because they lack ideas but because they lack clarity in making decisions. Thought leadership steps in by offering frameworks that move groups forward.

I once facilitated a team that debated endlessly. Meetings stretched on, but choices were delayed. Frustration grew, and opportunities slipped away. The team mistook discussion for progress.

In another setting, I watched a leader simplify decision-making by clarifying criteria upfront. He asked, 'What matters most in this choice—speed, cost, or quality?' That one question streamlined the entire process.

Clarity transforms decision-making from confusion into confidence. It doesn't eliminate debate, but it gives the team a shared lens for evaluating options.

Without clarity, decisions drag, and momentum dies. With clarity, even tough calls feel manageable, because the framework is visible and fair.

Thought leaders help teams make decisions not by dictating but by framing. They don't impose answers—they sharpen the questions.

This approach builds buy-in. People may not always agree with the outcome, but they respect the process because they saw the criteria clearly.

Over time, clear decision-making builds trust. Teams learn that debates won't spiral endlessly. They know a path forward will emerge.

What this shows is that leadership in decision-making is less about control and more about clarity. Leaders who provide frameworks empower teams to act with confidence.

The more you practice clarity in decisions, the more your team learns to move forward together instead of stalling apart.

Activity: In your next team decision, clarify the top 2–3 criteria before discussion. Notice how it changes the conversation.

Reflection: How does clarifying decision criteria strengthen your team's confidence in moving forward?

Day 69: Applying Thought Leadership in Business Teams

Innovation often feels like a buzzword, but in practice, it's about creating space for new ideas. Business teams suffocate innovation when they prize conformity over creativity. Thought leaders shift the culture by inviting experimentation.

I once joined a team where new ideas were quietly punished. Suggestions were met with silence or subtle criticism. Over time, people stopped sharing. The team grew stagnant, trapped in old routines.

In contrast, another leader encouraged even half-formed ideas. She celebrated attempts, not just results. By lowering the risk of speaking up, she multiplied the flow of creativity.

Innovation requires psychological safety. People must know they won't be ridiculed for trying. Without safety, potential breakthroughs stay locked inside hesitant minds.

Thought leadership creates that safety. It frames experiments as opportunities to learn, not tests to pass. It asks, 'What can we discover?' instead of, 'What if we fail?'

When teams adopt this mindset, they move faster. Even failed experiments teach them something valuable. Success becomes a process, not a rare event.

The best innovations often emerge from a chain of small ideas, each building on the last. That chain only forms when people feel free to contribute.

Over time, a culture of experimentation becomes a culture of growth. Teams stop fearing failure and start embracing possibility.

What this shows is that innovation isn't about genius moments—it's about everyday courage to suggest, to try, to learn. Leaders who make space for this unlock hidden potential.

The more your team feels safe to innovate, the more clarity you'll uncover about what works, what doesn't, and what's possible next.

Activity: Invite your team to share one experimental idea this week, no matter how small. Celebrate the effort, not just the outcome.

Reflection: How does creating space for experimentation shift your team's willingness to contribute new ideas?

Day 70: Applying Thought Leadership in Business Teams

Alignment is the invisible force that determines whether teams thrive or struggle. Without it, even talented groups feel stuck. With it, momentum flows naturally. Thought leaders help align people around shared goals and values.

I once worked with a team where each department had its own priorities. They clashed constantly, competing for resources instead of collaborating. The lack of alignment drained energy and slowed progress.

In another company, a leader made alignment a visible practice. At the start of projects, he asked, "How does this serve our mission?" That question pulled people out of silos and into shared purpose.

Alignment doesn't erase differences—it unites them under a bigger vision. It helps people see that their work connects to something meaningful and collective.

When alignment is absent, frustration grows. People feel like they're rowing in different directions. When alignment is present, effort compounds instead of colliding.

Thought leadership provides the compass for alignment. It reminds teams of the why behind the what. It translates strategy into daily focus.

This alignment also builds resilience. When challenges hit, teams that share purpose bend without breaking. Their unity helps them adapt without losing direction.

Leaders who prioritize alignment multiply energy. They show that clarity isn't just about individual tasks—it's about the harmony of the whole group.

What this shows is that alignment turns scattered efforts into synergy. Leaders who foster it transform disjointed activity into powerful collaboration.

The more you align your team's actions with shared purpose, the more sustainable and impactful your progress becomes.

Alignment also protects culture. A team may hit short-term goals without it, but over time misalignment erodes trust and drains morale. Shared purpose is what keeps people motivated to stay, contribute, and grow together.

It also sharpens decision-making. When teams are aligned, tough choices become clearer because everyone measures options against the same mission. Alignment simplifies complexity and reduces wasted debates.

And alignment fuels belonging. People want to know their efforts matter in the bigger picture. When leaders consistently connect individual work to shared purpose, team members feel part of something larger than themselves. That sense of belonging strengthens both performance and loyalty.

Day 71: Applying Thought Leadership in Community Leadership

Community leadership begins not with a microphone, but with listening. Too often, leaders assume they must have all the answers. But communities don't thrive when one voice dominates—they thrive when many voices are heard.

I once volunteered with a neighborhood group where the organizer spoke passionately but rarely asked questions. Meetings felt more like lectures than collaboration. Attendance dwindled because people didn't feel ownership.

In contrast, another community leader began every gathering with a simple question: 'What matters most to you right now?' That one practice transformed the tone of the group. People felt seen and valued.

Listening builds trust. When people sense their input matters, they invest more deeply. They bring energy, ideas, and solutions that no single leader could create alone.

Thought leadership in communities is about creating platforms, not pedestals. It's less about broadcasting and more about facilitating dialogue that reveals collective clarity.

This kind of leadership also prevents blind spots. Leaders who dominate conversations often miss critical issues simmering below the surface. Listening brings those hidden realities into the open.

Over time, consistent listening builds a culture of trust. People stop waiting for permission and start contributing freely. The community becomes self-sustaining because clarity is shared, not hoarded.

What this shows is that the strongest communities are not led by the loudest voice, but by the one who listens most carefully. Listening is not passive—it is active leadership.

The thought leader in a community doesn't pretend to know everything. They simply create a safe space where truth can surface and guide the way forward.

When you begin with listening, you multiply engagement. Clarity rises from the group itself, and people rally around it because they feel it is theirs.

Activity: In your next community gathering, ask one open-ended question and spend more time listening than speaking.

Reflection: How does creating space for listening change the energy of your community interactions?

Shared Wisdom, Shared Growth

Day 72: Applying Thought Leadership in Community Leadership

Communities thrive on connection. Without it, they fragment into isolated individuals. Thought leadership in communities means weaving threads of connection that bind people together in trust and purpose.

I once worked with a civic group that focused heavily on logistics—budgets, schedules, and policies. They were efficient but uninspired. Meetings felt transactional rather than relational.

Then a new leader introduced something small but powerful: sharing circles. At the start of each meeting, people took a few minutes to share a personal story or update. That practice humanized the group.

As people connected, energy shifted. Collaboration became easier because members now saw each other as people, not just roles. Trust grew, and new partnerships formed.

Connection turns strangers into allies. It builds resilience because people are less likely to disengage when they feel bonded to the group.

Thought leadership here isn't about efficiency—it's about empathy. It recognizes that communities move at the speed of trust, not at the pace of agendas.

Strong communities are built not only on shared goals but on shared humanity. When people feel connected, they stay, they contribute, and they grow together.

What this shows is that connection is not a luxury—it's the foundation of collective impact. Without it, communities collapse under pressure. With it, they thrive.

The leader's role is to nurture these bonds, ensuring that connection remains central, even as the group pursues ambitious goals.

The more you invest in connection, the stronger your community becomes—and the clearer its shared direction will be.

Activity: Introduce one practice this week that fosters connection in your community, such as sharing stories or check-ins.

Reflection: How does focusing on connection change the commitment of people in your community?

Day 73: Applying Thought Leadership in Community Leadership

Sustainable communities require shared ownership. When leadership rests on one person, the group is fragile. Thought leadership ensures responsibility is distributed so the community can endure.

I once joined a nonprofit where the founder handled everything—events, fundraising, communication. Her passion was unmatched, but the weight was unsustainable. When she burned out, the organization nearly collapsed.

In contrast, I saw another group thrive because its leader intentionally shared ownership. Committees were empowered, and decisions were made collectively. The result was not chaos but resilience.

Shared ownership doesn't dilute leadership—it multiplies it. People invest more when they feel responsibility for the outcome. The group becomes less dependent on one person and more capable as a whole.

This approach requires humility. Leaders must be willing to release control and trust others. But the payoff is enormous: stronger engagement, more innovation, and greater sustainability.

Communities with shared ownership also weather transitions better. When one leader steps away, the vision doesn't vanish because it lives in the group itself.

Thought leadership in this context means asking, 'Who else can carry this forward?' It's about cultivating capacity in others so the mission outlasts any individual.

What this shows is that shared ownership is not weakness—it's wisdom. Communities led this way grow deeper roots and wider branches.

The role of the leader is not to hold all the power but to create more leaders. That is the essence of sustainable thought leadership in communities.

When ownership is shared, the community not only survives—it thrives, fueled by collective clarity and commitment.

Activity: Identify one responsibility you currently hold alone. Share it with someone else in your community this week.

Reflection: How does shifting responsibility to others strengthen your community's resilience?

Day 74: Applying Thought Leadership in Community Leadership

Communities are shaped by stories. They define identity, inspire action, and preserve memory. Thought leadership in communities means curating and amplifying these stories to create shared meaning.

I once attended a local gathering where achievements were measured only by numbers—dollars raised, tasks completed. While informative, it felt sterile. People left uninspired because they didn't connect emotionally.

At another event, the leader invited members to share personal stories of how the group had impacted them. The atmosphere transformed. Tears, laughter, and renewed energy filled the room.

Stories remind communities why they exist. They carry values better than bullet points and inspire commitment better than statistics.

A thought leader knows which stories to highlight and how to frame them. They use stories not to manipulate but to magnify the truth of the community's purpose.

When stories are celebrated, members feel proud to belong. They see themselves as part of something larger, woven into a narrative that matters.

This storytelling also attracts others. People outside the group are drawn in by authentic accounts of transformation and belonging.

What this shows is that communities move not only on strategy but on story. Leaders who amplify stories strengthen both identity and impact.

The leader's job is not to invent stories but to notice them, to lift them up, and to connect them to the larger vision.

The more stories you share, the more your community will see itself clearly—and act with renewed purpose.

Activity: Collect one story from your community this week and share it publicly with others.

Reflection: How does amplifying stories change the way your community understands itself?

Day 75: Applying Thought Leadership in Community Leadership

Communities flourish when people feel they belong. Without belonging, participation fades. Thought leadership in communities means creating spaces where everyone knows they are valued and included.

I once visited a group where newcomers were barely acknowledged. The core members chatted with each other while outsiders sat quietly. Unsurprisingly, few visitors returned.

In another community, leaders trained members to welcome newcomers with warmth and curiosity. They paired them with mentors, making sure no one felt invisible. Retention soared because people felt they belonged.

Belonging is more than hospitality. It's the deep sense that 'I am part of this, and I matter here.' It cannot be faked—it must be cultivated consistently.

Communities that cultivate belonging see higher engagement, stronger commitment, and more resilience. People fight for spaces where they feel at home.

Thought leaders in this area understand that inclusion is not optional—it's essential. They design environments where every person, regardless of background, feels seen and valued.

Belonging also bridges differences. When people feel secure, they are more open to diverse perspectives. This strengthens the group's ability to innovate and adapt.

What this shows is that belonging is not a side benefit—it is the foundation of community strength. Without it, no strategy will hold. With it, communities endure and grow.

The leader's role is to ensure no one stands on the margins. Belonging must be intentional, baked into the culture of the group.

The more you build belonging, the stronger your community becomes—because people stay where they feel they are home.

Activity: Welcome one new or quiet member of your community personally this week. Learn their story and help them connect.

Reflection: How does creating belonging strengthen your community's long-term health and clarity?

Day 76: Applying Thought Leadership in Community Leadership

Leadership in communities often comes down to how well leaders can mobilize volunteers. Volunteers aren't motivated by paychecks; they're motivated by meaning. A thought leader recognizes this and builds environments where purpose is clear.

I once volunteered for a group where the leader treated us like employees. Tasks were handed out, but vision was never shared. Over time, volunteers dropped off, because the work felt like obligation instead of contribution.

In contrast, another organization I joined had a leader who constantly tied small tasks back to the larger mission. When I handed out flyers, she reminded me that each one represented a potential family finding support. That clarity fueled my commitment.

People give their best when they know why it matters. Purpose turns routine into meaning. It transforms effort into energy.

Thought leadership in volunteer-driven settings is about framing. Leaders frame every action in light of the bigger story. This keeps people engaged even in mundane work.

Volunteers aren't inspired by micromanagement—they're inspired by meaning. When clarity is offered consistently, commitment grows stronger.

This is why turnover is often a leadership issue, not a volunteer issue. When leaders fail to connect tasks to purpose, energy fades. When they succeed, people give more than expected.

What this shows is that mobilizing communities isn't about control—it's about clarity. It's about helping people see how their piece fits into the whole.

When volunteers understand the mission behind their actions, they carry the vision with pride. They see themselves not just as helpers, but as contributors to something lasting.

Your role as a thought leader is to make the invisible visible—to connect small efforts to the greater cause that sustains the community.

Activity: The next time you assign a task, explain why it matters in the larger mission of your community.

Reflection: How does connecting tasks to purpose shift the way people commit their time and energy?

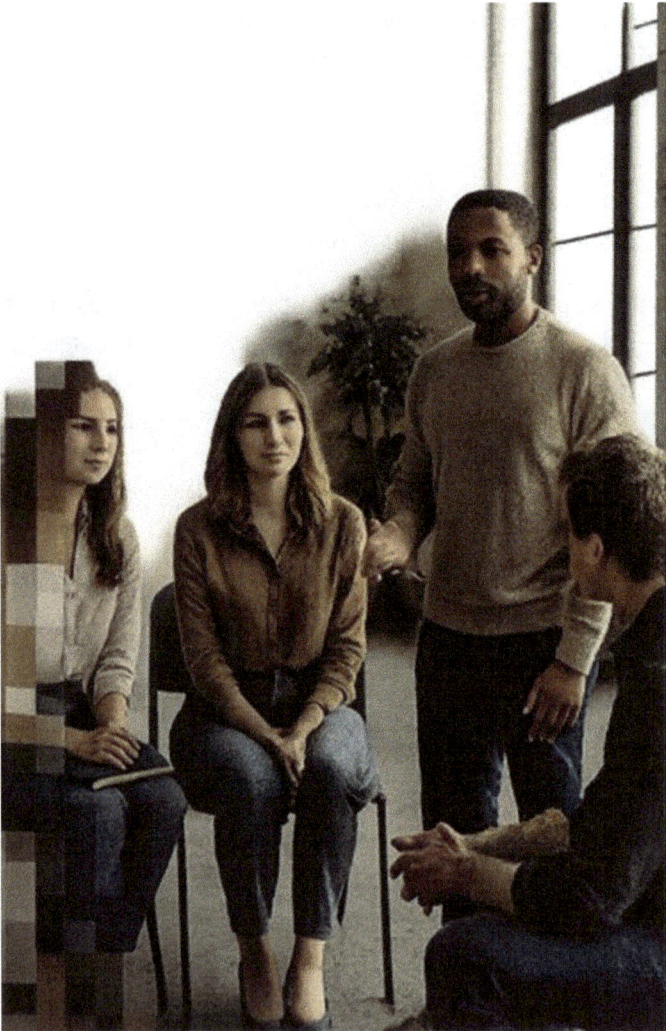

Day 77: Applying Thought Leadership in Community Leadership

Diversity is strength, but only if it is embraced. Communities often attract people from different backgrounds, skills, and perspectives. Thought leadership ensures those differences aren't just tolerated but celebrated.

I once attended community meetings where differences were brushed aside. Leaders rushed toward consensus without inviting diverse input. Important voices were lost, and the solutions were shallow.

In contrast, another community leader intentionally invited diverse perspectives. She asked for opinions from newcomers, young members, and even those who had disagreed in the past. The richness of ideas elevated the group's decisions.

Diversity without inclusion creates frustration. People may be present but silent. Inclusion turns diversity into innovation by making space for every voice.

Thought leaders know that clarity grows sharper when it is tested by different angles. They welcome disagreement as a way to refine ideas rather than a threat to unity.

Communities that embrace diversity are more adaptable. They see challenges from multiple lenses and craft stronger solutions. They are also more attractive to outsiders, who feel welcomed rather than excluded.

This requires humility. Leaders must let go of control and accept that the best answers may come from unexpected places. The community becomes wiser when its wisdom is shared broadly.

What this shows is that diversity is not just demographic—it is perspective. And when leaders include those perspectives, clarity expands for everyone.

The result is a culture where people don't just join the community— they belong in it, bringing their full selves to the table.

The more diversity is embraced, the more resilient and innovative the community becomes.

Activity: In your next community discussion, invite input from someone who is often quiet or overlooked.

Reflection: How does including diverse voices expand the clarity of your community's decisions?

Day 78: Applying Thought Leadership in Community Leadership

Communities thrive when they celebrate milestones together. Celebrations aren't just about marking time—they're about reinforcing identity and reminding people why they belong. Thought leadership brings rhythm to these moments.

I once joined a local group that rarely paused to celebrate. They moved from one project to the next with no acknowledgment of progress. Participation slowly dwindled, because members felt their contributions didn't matter.

In another community, the leader scheduled small celebrations regularly. Even modest wins were recognized. A completed cleanup, a successful fundraiser, a new member welcomed—each moment was honored.

These celebrations weren't extravagant, but they were meaningful. They reminded people of progress and created positive energy for the next challenge.

Celebration connects the present to the purpose. It says, "We are moving forward together, and it matters." Without it, work feels like drudgery. With it, work feels like part of a story worth telling.

Thought leaders understand that celebration is not distraction—it's reinforcement. It anchors clarity in memory and keeps momentum alive.

Communities that celebrate together grow tighter bonds. They remember victories together, and those memories fuel resilience when challenges come.

This is not about throwing parties—it's about acknowledging meaning. Even a simple thank-you circle can transform morale.

What this shows is that communities need ritual as much as they need strategy. Celebrations build culture, and culture sustains clarity.

The more you celebrate milestones, the more people will remember why they joined—and why they stay.

Celebration also fosters ownership. When individuals see their contributions recognized, they feel more invested in the mission. That ownership translates into higher engagement and stronger commitment.

It also creates continuity. Each celebration ties past achievements to future goals, reminding the group that progress is cumulative. This continuity helps people see they are building something larger than themselves.

And celebration nurtures joy. In challenging seasons, joy becomes fuel. Communities that know how to celebrate even small wins build resilience by choosing gratitude over discouragement. That joy is contagious, strengthening both spirit and unity.

Activity: Plan one small celebration for your community this week to honor a recent achievement.

Reflection: How does celebrating progress shift the energy and resilience of your community?

Day 79: Applying Thought Leadership in Community Leadership

Communication is the lifeline of communities. Without clear communication, even the most passionate groups fall into confusion. Thought leadership ensures that messages are consistent, transparent, and trustworthy.

I once worked with a community that struggled with rumors. Because leaders didn't communicate openly, misinformation spread faster than facts. Distrust grew, and unity suffered.

In another community, leaders prioritized transparent communication. They shared updates openly, admitted uncertainties, and invited questions. The result was not weakness but trust.

Clear communication prevents small issues from becoming crises. It builds confidence that leaders respect the community enough to keep them informed.

Thought leaders don't just broadcast—they dialogue. They make sure communication flows in both directions, giving members voice as well as updates.

When communication is strong, people feel secure. They know where things stand and what to expect. That clarity reduces anxiety and keeps focus on the mission.

Weak communication, by contrast, creates shadows. And in shadows, fear grows. Transparency is light—it reveals truth and builds resilience.

What this shows is that communication is more than logistics. It is a trust-building practice that sustains clarity and alignment.

Leaders who communicate with honesty and openness create communities that are harder to fracture because misinformation cannot take root.

The clearer and more transparent the communication, the stronger the bonds of trust and unity within the community.

Activity: Audit your current community communication. Identify one way to make it more transparent and consistent this week.

Reflection: How does clearer communication affect the trust and focus of your community?

Day 80: Applying Thought Leadership in Community Leadership

Sustainability is a challenge for many communities. Energy is often high at the beginning but fades over time. Thought leadership keeps sustainability alive by building rhythms, structures, and practices that outlast enthusiasm.

I once joined a community group that launched with excitement but quickly fizzled. They had no systems in place, and when initial passion waned, nothing kept momentum going.

In contrast, another group created simple structures. Rotating leadership roles, scheduled check-ins, and clear goals provided stability. Even when individuals cycled out, the group kept thriving.

Sustainability comes from discipline, not just inspiration. Passion ignites the flame, but structure keeps it burning.

Thought leaders know that enthusiasm must be matched with systems. They build habits into the community that make participation natural instead of forced.

This might look like monthly gatherings, annual retreats, or rotating committees. The specific form matters less than the consistency behind it.

Communities with sustainability don't collapse under transitions. They adapt, because their strength lies in shared clarity, not individual charisma.

What this shows is that long-term impact requires both energy and endurance. Leaders who prioritize sustainability leave a legacy rather than a flash in the pan.

Your role is not only to spark momentum but to sustain it. Sustainability ensures that clarity continues to serve even after you step away.

The stronger your systems of sustainability, the longer your community's clarity will shine into the future.

Activity: Identify one practice or rhythm you can add to your community that promotes long-term sustainability.

Reflection: How does building sustainability shift your community's confidence in its future?

Day 81: Applying Thought Leadership in Family Leadership

Family leadership begins at home, often in the smallest moments. It isn't about commanding authority—it's about creating clarity that strengthens bonds and nurtures growth. I once knew a father who rarely gave big speeches but always asked thoughtful questions at dinner. His children grew up confident in their ability to think and communicate clearly.

The mistake many make is assuming leadership in families must be grand gestures—rules, lectures, or dramatic interventions. In reality, it often shows up in consistent, intentional presence. Clarity lives in the rhythm of daily life.

I once worked with a young professional who said the best leadership she received came not from her boss but from her mother, who consistently modeled listening. By showing curiosity, her mother gave her the confidence to speak and the courage to lead herself.

Family leadership is thought leadership at its most personal. It doesn't rely on a stage or spotlight. It happens in living rooms, kitchens, and car rides. The clarity offered here shapes how people see themselves for life.

This influence multiplies across generations. Children raised in clarity grow into adults who lead with clarity. Families that practice listening and purpose don't just raise individuals—they build legacies.

The challenge is that family leadership is often invisible. There are no performance reviews or quarterly check-ins. The results appear years later, in the way children respond to challenges and relationships.

Thought leaders at home create environments where honesty is safe and learning is constant. They turn mistakes into lessons rather than punishments, helping family members grow resilient rather than fearful.

What this shows is that family leadership is not about perfection. It's about presence. It's about showing up with consistency, honesty, and care, even when life feels messy.

When families are led with clarity, they become safe havens where people recharge, refocus, and rediscover purpose before returning to the wider world.

Your role at home is to make clarity a habit, so your family sees leadership not as control but as care, not as rules but as guidance.

Activity: Ask one thoughtful question at your next family meal that invites reflection instead of small talk.

Reflection: How does creating space for meaningful dialogue shift the atmosphere of your family time?

Day 82: Applying Thought Leadership in Family Leadership

Respect is the foundation of family leadership. Without it, relationships fracture. With it, families flourish. I once counseled a teenager who said, 'I know my parents love me, but I don't think they respect me.' The absence of respect left her feeling unseen and unheard.

In contrast, another family I observed practiced respect intentionally. Parents valued their children's opinions, even when they disagreed. They created space for dialogue instead of shutting it down. The result was not chaos but trust.

Respect at home doesn't mean lack of boundaries. It means boundaries are set with clarity and mutual understanding rather than force or fear.

When respect is modeled consistently, family members carry it into their relationships outside the home. They learn to value others and themselves in ways that strengthen every part of their lives.

Thought leadership in families is about showing that respect is not earned by age or authority—it is given as a basic posture of care. From respect, influence grows naturally.

Without respect, even well-intentioned leadership feels like control. With respect, even correction feels like guidance rather than punishment.

Respect also creates resilience. Families built on respect can handle conflict better because disagreements don't threaten belonging. They become opportunities to understand rather than battles to win.

What this shows is that respect is not an accessory—it is the foundation. Without it, no leadership approach will last. With it, clarity has fertile ground to grow.

Family leaders who practice respect daily plant seeds of trust that grow into lifelong confidence in those they guide.

When respect is present, families become training grounds for the kind of leadership the world desperately needs.

Activity: This week, intentionally affirm one family member's perspective, even if you disagree with it.

Reflection: How does offering respect in moments of difference strengthen your family relationships?

Day 83: Applying Thought Leadership in Family Leadership

Conflict at home can be some of the most challenging to navigate, because emotions run deeper and bonds are closer. But it is also where clarity can do the most good. I once witnessed a family where conflict meant shouting and avoidance. The pattern left wounds that took years to heal.

In another family, conflict was embraced as an opportunity. Parents modeled calm discussion even when they disagreed. Children learned that differences weren't disasters but invitations to understand.

Thought leadership in family conflict isn't about pretending tension doesn't exist. It's about guiding it toward understanding and growth. It's about reframing conflict as connection, not division.

One parent I knew taught their children to pause before reacting by asking, 'What do you need right now?' That simple question shifted arguments into conversations and reduced escalation.

Families that embrace this approach build resilience. Children grow confident in their ability to face tension without fear. Spouses learn to support each other through difficulty rather than withdraw.

The absence of conflict doesn't mean health—it often means silence. Health comes from learning to disagree with love and resolve with clarity.

Thought leaders at home don't run from conflict. They lean into it with patience, modeling skills that children will carry into workplaces, friendships, and future families.

What this shows is that conflict can either fracture or forge. The difference lies in whether clarity is brought into the moment.

When families navigate conflict with clarity, bonds strengthen instead of weakening. Disagreements become opportunities to deepen trust.

Leadership at home means turning even hard conversations into chances for connection and growth.

Activity: The next time conflict arises, ask one clarifying question instead of defending your position.

Reflection: How does reframing conflict at home change the way your family experiences tension?

Day 84: Applying Thought Leadership in Family Leadership

Traditions carry enormous weight in families. They anchor identity, create memories, and reinforce values. Thought leadership in families means shaping traditions intentionally so they communicate clarity about what matters most.

I once visited a family where traditions were only about routine— holiday meals, birthdays, and nothing more. They were pleasant but empty, disconnected from meaning. The children grew up with memories but little sense of shared purpose.

In another family, traditions were woven with intention. Weekly dinners became moments of gratitude. Holiday gatherings included storytelling about ancestors. These traditions weren't elaborate, but they carried deep clarity about values.

Traditions remind families of who they are. They reinforce belonging and identity. Done well, they become compasses that guide members long after they leave home.

Thought leadership here is about asking: what story are our traditions telling? Are they teaching our values, or are they just filling time?

Families that lead with clarity choose traditions that strengthen purpose. They make sure rituals aren't just repeated, but remembered for their meaning.

This doesn't require creating new traditions from scratch. It can be as simple as infusing existing ones with intentionality—adding a moment of gratitude, reflection, or storytelling.

When traditions are clear, they build resilience. They remind families of continuity and connection, even during times of change.

What this shows is that traditions are not trivial—they are tools. Leaders at home use them to pass on clarity and values to future generations.

The more intentional you are with traditions, the more your family will experience them as anchors of meaning rather than just moments on a calendar.

Activity: Add one intentional element to an existing family tradition this week, such as gratitude or storytelling.

Reflection: How do intentional traditions shape the clarity and values of your family?

Day 85: Applying Thought Leadership in Family Leadership

Families thrive when love is visible. It's easy to assume family members know they are loved, but without consistent demonstration, uncertainty creeps in. Leadership at home requires turning love into clarity through action.

I once spoke with an adult who said, 'I know my parents loved me, but they rarely showed it.' The lack of visible love left gaps in confidence that lingered into adulthood.

In contrast, I knew another family where love was expressed often— through words, touch, and time. The children carried deep assurance into their adult lives. They didn't question their worth because it had been reinforced daily.

Love in families is not just emotion—it is practice. It's the clarity of showing, not just saying. It's the consistency of demonstrating care in ways that resonate with each member.

Thought leadership in families ensures love is part of the culture, not an occasional event. It makes sure no one in the home doubts their place or their value.

Visible love also strengthens resilience. Families that express care openly weather challenges better because affection builds security that stress cannot easily shake.

This doesn't mean perfection. It means persistence—choosing to show love daily, even in small gestures. Consistency matters more than extravagance.

When families lead with visible love, they model healthy relationships for children, who carry those practices into friendships, workplaces, and future families.

What this shows is that leadership at home begins with love. It transforms homes into places of trust, healing, and growth.

The clearer love is expressed, the more powerful its impact will be across a lifetime.

Activity: Show love visibly to one family member today through words, actions, or presence.

Reflection: How does demonstrating love consistently change the atmosphere of your family?

Day 86: Applying Thought Leadership in Family Leadership

Guidance in families is often expressed through boundaries. Without boundaries, families drift into chaos. With them, they provide structure that fosters safety and growth. Thought leadership at home means setting boundaries with clarity and compassion.

I once observed a family where rules were enforced harshly, with little explanation. Children complied out of fear but grew resentful. The boundaries created order but not trust.

In another family, parents explained the reasons behind their boundaries. They invited questions, even if the rules remained firm. The result was not rebellion but respect. Children understood the purpose, and clarity reduced conflict.

Boundaries should not be walls that trap, but guardrails that guide. They provide freedom within safe limits, allowing family members to explore without losing direction.

Thought leaders in families understand that clarity matters as much as consistency. Boundaries that are unclear confuse. Boundaries that are inconsistent frustrate. But boundaries explained and applied fairly build trust.

Over time, these kinds of boundaries create security. Family members know where they stand, and uncertainty doesn't erode relationships.

Clarity in boundaries also prepares children for life beyond home. They learn to respect limits while still exercising independence. They carry these lessons into schools, workplaces, and relationships.

What this shows is that healthy families balance freedom with structure. Leadership in this context is less about control and more about stewardship of trust and safety.

Boundaries guided by clarity protect not only behavior but relationships. They turn family rules into lessons of love rather than instruments of fear.

When boundaries are clear, consistent, and compassionate, families thrive—and every member learns how to lead themselves well.

Activity: Review one family boundary this week. Explain its purpose clearly to your family members and invite their thoughts.

Reflection: How does adding clarity to a boundary change the way it is received and respected at home?

Day 87: Applying Thought Leadership in Family Leadership

Encouragement is a powerful form of leadership in families. It is more than praise—it is the art of naming potential and reinforcing effort. I once worked with a young adult who said, 'The only reason I kept trying was because my grandmother always told me she believed in me.'

Encouragement is not empty flattery. It points out real progress, even if small. It says, 'I see you growing, and I believe you can go further.' That kind of clarity inspires perseverance.

In families without encouragement, discouragement fills the void. Silence in the face of effort can feel like disapproval. Over time, it weakens confidence and motivation.

Thought leaders at home make encouragement a habit. They look for opportunities daily to recognize effort and potential, not just outcomes.

Encouragement is also about timing. A single word spoken in a moment of doubt can change the trajectory of someone's decision. Families thrive when encouragement is present at the right moments.

Encouragement multiplies resilience. It helps family members face challenges with courage because they carry the memory of someone believing in them.

The opposite is also true—criticism without encouragement erodes confidence. Families that critique more than they encourage breed insecurity instead of growth.

What this shows is that encouragement is not optional. It is essential fuel for development and clarity. It doesn't take long speeches, only consistent reminders that growth is seen and valued.

When families practice encouragement, they create cultures of resilience. They raise members who are not afraid to try, fail, and try again.

Encouragement at home plants seeds of confidence that grow into strong leaders beyond the family circle.

Activity: Encourage one family member today by naming a specific strength or effort you see in them.

Reflection: How does intentional encouragement shift the confidence of your family members?

Day 88: Applying Thought Leadership in Family Leadership

Resilience in families comes not from avoiding hardship but from navigating it together. Challenges are inevitable, but clarity in leadership helps families face them with strength.

I once knew a family that faced financial hardship. Instead of hiding the struggle, the parents shared openly in age-appropriate ways. They explained the situation, involved the children in solutions, and reminded them of their shared values.

The result was not despair but unity. The children grew up with resourcefulness and resilience because they had been trusted with clarity instead of left in confusion.

In another family, hardship was hidden. Parents shielded children from reality, but the silence bred fear and insecurity. Without clarity, uncertainty became more frightening than the hardship itself.

Thought leadership in resilience is about honesty matched with hope. It doesn't sugarcoat challenges, but it frames them within a narrative of possibility and purpose.

Families that practice resilience model adaptability. They show that while circumstances may be hard, their values remain steady. This consistency reassures every member.

Resilience also grows when families celebrate progress along the way. Even small wins in hard times reinforce the belief that challenges can be overcome.

What this shows is that resilience is less about circumstances and more about clarity. Families led with honesty and hope learn to thrive even in difficulty.

Children raised in such environments become adults who carry resilience into every sphere of life, from careers to communities.

Resilient families leave a legacy of strength. Their clarity in hardship becomes the model for generations that follow.

Activity: Share one honest story of how your family overcame a past challenge. Highlight the values that carried you through.

Reflection: How does remembering resilience in the past shape your family's confidence for the future?

Day 89: Applying Thought Leadership in Family Leadership

Gratitude is a powerful force in family leadership. It shifts attention from what is missing to what is present. Families that practice gratitude regularly develop clarity about what truly matters.

I once stayed with a family that ended every day by sharing something they were thankful for. It was a simple ritual, but it transformed the atmosphere of the home. Even during stressful weeks, gratitude anchored them.

Gratitude is contagious. When leaders model it, others adopt it. It shifts conversations from complaint to appreciation, from scarcity to abundance.

In families where gratitude is absent, dissatisfaction grows. People focus on flaws and frustrations, which erodes joy and connection.

Thought leadership in gratitude is about cultivating perspective. It reminds families that even when life isn't perfect, there is much to celebrate and cherish.

Gratitude also strengthens resilience. Families that give thanks together find it easier to endure difficulties, because they have trained their eyes to see goodness even in hard times.

This practice builds bonds. Family members who feel appreciated are more likely to show appreciation in return, creating a cycle of positivity.

What this shows is that gratitude doesn't erase problems, but it reframes them. It shifts the story families tell themselves about their lives.

When gratitude becomes a rhythm, it sustains clarity about what matters most: relationships, growth, and shared love.

The clearer gratitude is expressed, the stronger the family becomes in both joy and struggle.

Activity: Start a gratitude ritual this week by inviting each family member to name one thing they are thankful for.

Reflection: How does practicing gratitude together change the way your family views daily life?

Day 90: Applying Thought Leadership in Family Leadership

Legacy is the final lesson of family leadership. Every family passes something on—values, habits, stories. Thought leadership ensures that what is passed on is intentional and rooted in clarity.

I once spoke with an adult who said, "The most important thing my parents gave me was their integrity." They didn't leave wealth or possessions, but they left a model of honesty and consistency that shaped her life.

In contrast, others inherit confusion—mixed messages, unresolved conflict, or unspoken pain. These legacies ripple across generations, often without being questioned.

Thought leadership asks: what do we want our family to carry forward? It shapes daily actions with the awareness that they are building a legacy for tomorrow.

Legacy is not built in big moments. It is built in the daily choices that accumulate into a family story—choices about honesty, kindness, perseverance, and respect.

When families lead with clarity, their legacy is one of trust and love. That legacy equips future generations with a compass for navigating life's challenges.

Legacy also multiplies. Families who model clarity influence not only their children but their communities, workplaces, and beyond.

What this shows is that leadership at home is never just about the present. It is about the ripple effect of values carried into the future.

Clarity ensures the legacy is not accidental but intentional. It makes sure what is passed on builds rather than burdens.

The legacy you leave will not be measured only in possessions, but in the clarity, values, and love you instill.

Legacy is also a story. Families that take time to share stories—of challenges overcome, lessons learned, and values lived—pass on more than principles. They pass on identity. Stories give flesh to values, making them memorable and repeatable for future generations.

It is also a mirror. The legacy you're building reflects your daily choices back to you, asking: are these habits, words, and actions worth passing on? That mirror can be uncomfortable, but it is also an invitation to grow and realign.

And legacy is a gift. Unlike possessions, it cannot be lost or taken away. A clear legacy of love, honesty, or resilience equips future generations with tools they can carry anywhere, into any season of life.

What stories from your family past have most shaped who you are today?

Which values do you want to continue—and which cycles do you want to break?

How do your daily choices reflect the legacy you want to leave?

What rituals or practices could you introduce to strengthen your family's sense of identity?

If someone asked your children or loved ones about your legacy 20 years from now, what would you want them to say?

[Write here]

_____

_____

_____

_____

Conclusion: Beyond the First 90 Days

Reaching the end of ninety days isn't the end of your journey—it's the proof that your journey has truly begun. These first steps have shown you what's possible when clarity, content, and community come together. But the question now is simple: what happens next?

Too many people treat milestones like finish lines. They celebrate, then stop. The truth is, your ninety-day mark isn't a finish line—it's a launchpad. You've built momentum. Now is the time to use it.

Think of it like training for a race. The first ninety days are the warm-up. They build stamina, discipline, and rhythm. But the real race—the one that changes your life—begins after you've proven you can keep going.

Leaders who stop at ninety days fade back into the noise. Leaders who continue beyond ninety days turn their spark into a flame. They become voices others depend on, not just for inspiration, but for guidance.

Reflection: Pause here and ask yourself—what do I want the next ninety days to look like? What would it mean if I doubled down on the habits I've built?

The next phase of thought leadership is expansion. You've clarified your genius, shaped your story, built your engine, and engaged your community. Now you amplify. You keep going, not with fireworks, but with steady light.

I've seen countless leaders reach their ninety-day milestone and hesitate. They wonder if they've shared too much, if their audience will get bored, if they have anything left to say. The truth? Most people are just starting to notice you.

Consistency compounds. The work you've done so far has laid the foundation. The work you do next cements it.

Think of momentum like a snowball rolling downhill. The first push is the hardest. But once it's rolling, gravity does the rest. Your ninety days were the push. Now you get to enjoy the acceleration.

This is also the moment to revisit clarity. Your story will evolve as you grow. The narrative that worked at day one may not fit at day ninety. That's okay. Thought leadership is alive, and living things grow.

Reflection: Write down three ways your clarity has shifted since day one. How have your words, your focus, or your energy changed?

Beyond ninety days, the cycle repeats. Clarity leads to content. Content creates community. Community builds credibility. Credibility strengthens clarity. The circle keeps turning, each rotation gaining more force.

The leaders who thrive are the ones who embrace the cycle. They don't expect a single post, milestone, or launch to do all the work. They build, repeat, refine, and expand.

I once worked with a client who committed to ninety days of content. At the milestone, she hosted a small webinar. Only twenty people attended. But she didn't stop there. She repeated the process. By the next cycle, it was fifty people. By the third, it was two hundred. Consistency turned small ripples into waves.

Another leader reached day ninety with a blog that had a modest but loyal readership. Instead of pausing, he turned his articles into a book manuscript. That book went on to open doors he never imagined. Ninety days was just the seed.

Your story can unfold the same way. These habits aren't temporary—they're the building blocks of your leadership journey.

Reflection: Ask yourself—what's the bigger story you want your ninety days to tell? Not just now, but a year from now, or five years from now?

The danger of ninety days is complacency. Don't confuse achievement with arrival. Arrival doesn't exist in leadership—it's a process, not a place.

Remember the metaphor from the beginning: fireworks versus lighthouses. Fireworks fade. Lighthouses endure. Ninety days can feel like fireworks, but the true test is whether you're willing to become a lighthouse.

Lighthouses don't shout. They don't sparkle. They shine steadily, night after night. They guide ships not with noise, but with clarity. That's the role of a thought leader beyond ninety days.

So don't stop now. Double down on what you've learned. Keep showing up. Keep refining your message. Keep amplifying your community.

If you ever feel doubt creeping in, remember: you've already proven you can do this. Ninety days is evidence. The only question is, will you keep going?

The world doesn't need another loud voice that fades after a burst of noise. It needs steady signals. It needs clarity, trust, and presence. It needs you.

Reflection: Write one commitment to yourself for the next ninety days. Keep it simple. Keep it clear. Let it be your lighthouse.

As you move forward, carry this truth with you: leadership isn't about one moment. It's about many moments, repeated with care and consistency.

Beyond the first ninety days lies the real work. The real influence. The real opportunity. You've built the foundation—now build the legacy.

The first ninety days were about proving you could start. The next ninety are about proving you can continue. And the cycle never ends. That's the beauty of it.

So keep shining. Keep building. Keep leading. Because the world is waiting for the signal only you can give.

About the Author

Bryon Casler didn't set out to become a thought leader. He set out to solve problems. From his earliest days in finance and operations, he noticed something others often overlooked: people were drowning in noise when what they needed was clarity.

That realization became a theme across his career. Whether he was building custom software for a fast-growing e-commerce business or designing data systems for nonprofits, Bryon always gravitated toward the same mission—simplifying complexity so others could focus on what mattered most.

His journey wasn't a straight line. Like many leaders, Bryon wore too many hats early on. At one point, his résumé listed six different titles. To outsiders, it looked impressive. To insiders, it was confusing. Even Bryon admits he wasn't sure which hat truly fit.

The turning point came when a mentor challenged him to cross out five of those titles. At first, the exercise felt painful. Each role represented years of hard work. But when he chose the one title that best reflected his genius, everything became clear. People finally understood his story. And more importantly, so did he.

From that moment, Bryon built his career around clarity. He designed processes that reduced twenty-eight hours of manual work down to two. He automated accounting systems that once overwhelmed teams. He trained leaders to cut through jargon and speak plainly so their people could act quickly and confidently.

Along the way, Bryon discovered that clarity isn't just about efficiency. It's about trust. Teams trusted him because he made things simple. Leaders trusted him because he told the truth, even when it was uncomfortable. Clients trusted him because he delivered results they could measure.

Outside of his professional life, Bryon carried the same mindset into community work. He founded initiatives that focused on creating value for people who often felt overlooked. He believed then, as he does now, that leadership isn't about being the loudest voice—it's about being the clearest signal.

Today, Bryon is known not just for his accomplishments, but for his philosophy: clarity is the most powerful form of leadership. It doesn't require charisma or titles. It requires honesty, consistency, and the courage to keep things simple.

Readers of this book will recognize those traits throughout the pages. The stories, the reflections, and the exercises all come from lessons Bryon learned firsthand—sometimes through success, often through mistakes. He doesn't write as a guru. He writes as a guide.

Reflection: Pause here and consider your own story. Like Bryon, you may find that the turning points came not when you added more hats, but when you chose the one that fit best.

Bryon lives in Jacksonville, North Carolina, where he continues to balance his professional leadership with personal commitments to family and community. His journey is still unfolding, and he sees this book not as the final word, but as an open invitation for others to step into their own clarity.

Because at the end of the day, Bryon believes the same thing he did when he automated that first system years ago: leadership isn't about doing more—it's about making what matters most easier for everyone else. And that's a message worth sharing.

Back Cover Blurb

In 90 days, you will cut through the noise, build clarity, and step confidently into thought leadership.

This playbook isn't theory—it's a structured, actionable guide with reflection journals, practical steps, and a framework that transforms leadership from vague aspiration into daily clarity.

Whether you're leading a team, a family, or yourself, this book gives you the tools to:
• Break free from overwhelm and confusion
• Focus on what truly matters in your leadership journey
• Create habits and actions that leave a lasting legacy

The 90-Day Thought Leader is your roadmap to becoming the voice of clarity in a noisy world.

www.ingramcontent.com/pod-product-compliance
Lightning Source LLC
Chambersburg PA
CBHW060529210326
41519CB00014B/3173